DISCARDED

C.1

$17.95

636.089
Run      Rundquist, Eric M.
         Reptile and amphibian
         parasites

MEDIALOG INC
ALEXANDRIA KY 41001

# Reptile and Amphibian Parasites

Eric M. Rundquist

Published in association with T.F.H. Publications, Inc.,
the world's largest and most respected publisher of pet literature

Chelsea House Publishers
Philadelphia

## CONTENTS

# Basic Domestic Reptile and Amphibian Library

Box Turtles
Lizards
Green Iguanas and Other Igaunids
Reptile and Amphibian Parasites
Newts
Snakes
Tarantulas and Scorpions
Chameleons
Tortoises

**Publisher's Note:** All of the photographs in this book have been coated with FOTOGLAZE™ finish, a special lamination that imparts a new dimension of colorful gloss to the photographs.

Reinforced Library binding & Super-Highest Quality Boards

This edition ©1999 Chelsea House Publishers, a division of Main Line Book Company.

Library of Congress Cataloging-in-Publication Data applied for 0-7910-5080-7

Library of Congress Cataloging-in-Publication Data

Rundquist, Eric M.
    Reptile & amphibian parasites / Eric M. Rundquist.
    p.     cm. — (Reptiles and amphibians)
    Includes index.
    Summary: Presents information about the different kinds of parasites found on pets and the illnesses they may cause; then offers suggestions on how to diagnose and combat the problem.
    ISBN 0-7910-5080-7 (hc)
    1. Reptiles—Parasites—Juvenile literature.
    2. Amphibians—Parasites—Juvenile literature.
    3. Veterinary parasitology—Juvenile literature.    [1. Reptiles.    2. Amphibians.
    3. Parasites.    4. Animals—Diseases.] I. Title. II. Series.
    SF997.5.R4L85 1998
    636.089'696—dc21

          98-22376
          CIP
          AC

# INTRODUCTION

Of the discrete illnesses that afflict amphibians and reptiles, parasitism is perhaps the one most frequently encountered in captives. Herps are host to an astounding array of various organisms that make their living off the bodies of other creatures. These parasites range from simple one-celled organisms to relatively complex creatures such as flies,

susceptible to parasitic disease. I have seen some rather remarkable infections in specimens which I had been assured were long-term captives that had received regular veterinary attention.

The following booklet contains information that may help you determine what sorts of parasites your pets may be harboring, what kind of illnesses these parasites

ISABELLE FRANCAIS, COURTESY OF BILL AND MARCIA BRANT

Shown is a beautiful "Miami Phase" Corn Snake, *Elaphe guttata guttata,* the product of carefully selected parents in a captive breeding program. It should be noted that an animal that has been captive-bred will not automatically be free of parasites. Many such animals are undoubtedly "cleaner," but not immune.

and the diseases they cause can have effects ranging from simple diarrhea to death. Although these critters are most frequently found in wild-caught captives (I doubt that there is such as a thing as a wild frog or snake that isn't carrying some sort of parasite), don't assume that just because you have a 12th-generation captive-bred Corn Snake, *Elaphe guttata,* the animal is not

may cause, signs that may help your veterinarian diagnose the parasite, and suggested regimes to combat the little buggers. Please understand that I am not a veterinarian, although I have been trained in parasite identification and diagnosis and spent some 12 years in the zoo business putting up with the illnesses these beasts cause. Drugs, dosages, and treatment schedules contained

ISABELLE FRANCAIS, COURTESY OF TOM CRUTCHFIELD

Captive-breeding programs are undoubtedly a channel through which top-quality animals, like this stunning pair of Blotched Bluetongue Skinks, *Tiliqua nigrolutea*, can be obtained, but further measures must then be taken by the keeper to maintain the necessary high standards. Such measures include a proper diet, proper climate replication, and constant cleaning of enclosures.

herein are only my suggestions; you should always work with a veterinarian in undertaking any course of medical treatment for your captives. Although many vets may not have direct experience in herp veterinary medicine, they are thoroughly trained in proper parasite diagnosis and treatment and are the only ones who should administer drugs and attempt any other sorts of treatments. You should never undertake such procedures on your own, as you will almost assuredly cause more harm than good. The first rule of veterinary medicine is to do no harm. That's a pretty good rule for life, also.

## DEDICATION

To my friend and colleague, Dr. William M. Bryant DVM, the hardest-working and most conscientious public servant I know.

## ACKNOWLEDGMENTS

Barbara Baumeister, veterinary technician at the Oklahoma City Zoo, was the first person to help refine my interest in herpetological parasitology and to instruct me in modern diagnostic methods. My good friend and colleague, David Grow, also of Oklahoma City Zoo, was an advisor and compadre in my early efforts to come to grips with the various creepy-crawlies to which amphibians and reptiles are host. Dr. William Bryant, Dr. Michael Renner DVM, Rosie Delgado, and Jenny Jenkins all of or formerly of the Sedgwick County Zoo, Wichita, Kansas have all been sources of considerable information and inspiration on technique, drug regimes, diagnosis, and parasite identification for nearly ten years. Their help and advice and debates have figured greatly in my current understanding and knowledge of herp parasites. All these people have my deep gratitude. Any errors of omission or commission herein are strictly my own.

# BACKGROUND AND BASICS

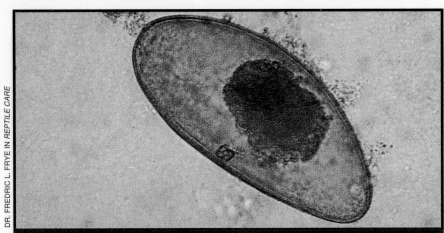

Shown is a plant mite ovum found in a Haitian Rhinoceros Iguana, *Cyclura ricordi*, that was maintained on an almost wholly vegetarian diet. It should be noted that although such items sometimes are ingested by herptiles, they are *not* considered internal parasites.

*DR. FREDRIC L. FRYE IN REPTILE CARE*

Herp parasites can be defined very broadly into two groups: external (ecto-) and internal (endo-) parasites. Ectoparasites are almost invariably arthropods; mites to mosquitoes. They rarely cause serious illness but can be indicators of poor husbandry practices. Endoparasites are the ones that cause the most serious disease and display the most variety of form. Of ectoparasites, mites of various kinds are the parasites most frequently seen and the ones that cause keepers the most headaches. Rarer external parasites are leeches, flies, fly larvae, ticks, and

Ticks are among the most common external parasites, or *ectoparasites*, found on herptiles, but most can be removed easily enough with a firm, steady hand and a pair of tweezers. Shown is a *Hyalomma aegyptium* latched onto a Greek Tortoise, *Testudo graeca*.

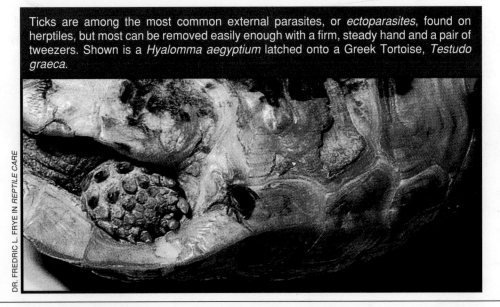

*DR. FREDRIC L. FRYE IN REPTILE CARE*

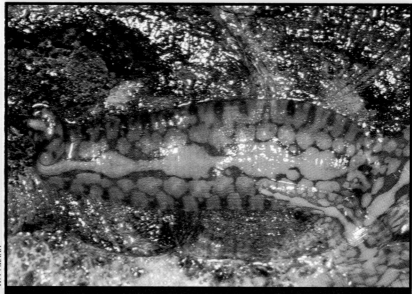

W. P. MARA

Leeches are commonly found on aquatic turtles, and often do not seem to cause the turtles any great harm. Some leeches, like the one shown, are attractively patterned and colored.

mosquitoes. I mention mosquitoes only in passing in that, although they do affect many kinds of amphibians and reptiles, they are not a concern unless you are maintaining your charges outside. Even then, I doubt there is anything you can do about them, but you should be aware that mosquitoes are vectors (carriers) for certain internal parasites that may do a great deal of damage to some of your pets.

On the other hand, endoparasites, by and large, will cause some sort of disease in your animals, and some of these illnesses are quite serious and can be devastating to large collections. Once again, very broadly, endoparasites divide into two groups: single-celled organisms (protozoans), and worms (although these creatures rarely resemble the earthworms

with which most folks are familiar). The medically important single-celled organisms are found in the blood system or digestive tract. Certain kinds may also invade other organ systems, but these parasites are rare and little is known about what kind of diseases they may cause.

Worms are generally found in the lungs, digestive tract, liver, or kidneys. However, they can be found in virtually any organ in your herp's body. A complicating factor with worms is the kind of life cycle they undergo. Many worms have what is called a direct life cycle; that is, they are passed from host to host directly, by the host ingesting eggs, larvae, or adults of these worms. These kinds of worms are the ones most frequently diagnosed and cause the major kinds of illness in herps.

Other worms (such as tapeworms and flukes) undergo what is called an indirect life cycle, meaning intermediate stages of these parasites must invade another host (or hosts) before that host is consumed and the parasite undergoes a transformation into an adult worm in the final host. Here is an example of a simple kind of indirect parasite—some fluke eggs hatch in a pond and attach themselves to underwater vegetation for a short time. A frog, escaping a predator at the water's surface, swims down to where these larvae are attached. The larvae sense that the frog is nearby and immediately swim to it and burrow into its skin. There, they undergo another transformation or two as a cyst and then go into a quiescent phase. The frog, unfortunately, does not escape the next predator to come along—a mink. After the mink has consumed the frog and digests it, the encysted fluke larvae escape from their cysts and burrow into the intestinal lining of the mink and into its blood system. From there, they migrate to the liver, where they undergo a final transformation into an adult fluke, which soon begins making and releasing eggs. These eggs enter the bile duct and then the intestine, where they are passed in the feces. If the eggs are passed in water, they hatch and wait to start the cycle all over again. Many kinds of amphibians and reptiles are prime intermediate

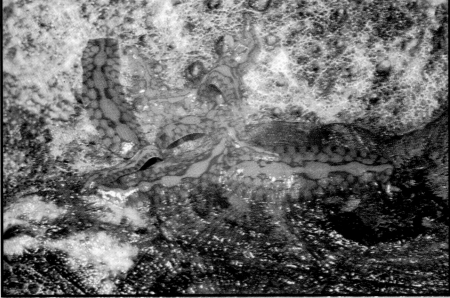

When acquiring a wild-caught aquatic turtle of any kind, a keeper should always make a point of carefully inspecting the animal for leeches. This small cluster, for example, was discovered on the belly of a large Alligator Snapper, *Macroclemmys temmincki*, that had been obtained by the photographer, W. P. Mara, in a pet shop. Bathing the turtle in a weak salt/water solution for a few hours each day for a period of about one week usually eradicates a leech problem.

hosts for worms with indirect life cycles. However, again, little is known about what, if any, disease these larval forms may cause in herps, so diagnosis is virtually impossible. On the other hand, herps are also the final hosts for many of these kinds of parasites, and diagnoses can be made and treatments instituted.

In the following pages, I will attempt to define the major · disease-causing herp parasites, indicate whether they have a direct or indirect life cycle, indicate their degree of pathogenicity (ability to cause disease), show how to diagnose the parasite, and suggest possible treatments. Some of these parasites, mites in particular, have a direct relationship to the degree of cleanliness that you practice with your pets. Let me emphasize that your basic

husbandry practices can have as much effect on the health of your animals as such disease-causing entities such as parasites. In this business, cleanliness is godliness, to quote a friend of mine. Practice good husbandry, and you probably will have very few problems with your animals.

## THE IMPORTANCE OF QUARANTINE

I highly recommend that you quarantine your animals for at least 30 days (preferably 60) before you place them in with the rest of your collection. The quarantine area should be completely away from the rest of your collection. This quarantine period will allow you to assess the health of your newcomers and will reduce the possibility of introducing disease to your other pets. During the quarantine period, you should collect at least

When quarantining any sick or newly acquired animal, put emphasis on simplicity of housing design. You will want to concentrate on careful observation of the animal rather than worry about things like the condition of live plants or the cleaning out of messy substrate materials.

ISABELLE FRANCAIS, COURTESY OF BILL AND MARCIA BRANT

ISABELLE FRANCAIS, COURTESY OF CHARLES AND MERILYN ABBOTT

Many reptile and amphibian parasites easily can be passed along by the keeper, so wash your hands between the handling of individual animals.

three fecal samples for testing from your new acquisition and all three should be negative before introducing the new animal to the standard collection. Chances are (especially if the animal is from the wild) that your vet will find some kind of parasite that must be treated before releasing the animal from quarantine. (NOTE: You should always service your quarantine specimens after you have worked with your regular collection. This significantly reduces disease transmission possibilities.) Once you have gotten three negative samples, the animal may join your other herps. If it has tested positive during quarantine, you should test it every three months for one year until you get consistent negative results. Certain parasites do not always show up, even during extended quarantine. All animals

in your group should have routine fecal exams twice a year.

**GOOD CLEANING HABITS**
As noted, cleaning and disinfection are paramount. To wit, if your animal poops, clean it up as soon as possible. If it spills its water bowl, clean it up. Use relatively sterile materials for substrates, such as newspaper for reptiles and clean smooth gravel or moist sphagnum moss for amphibians. Any soiled substrates should be removed and replaced and the soiled areas disinfected. For reptiles, a good general disinfectant is 2 ounces of bleach per gallon of water. This solution may also be used for amphibians, but be sure the animals have been moved from their enclosure and that the unit is thoroughly rinsed with very hot water afterwards and the unit

allowed to dry for at least 24 hours. There are a number of other disinfectants available and I would suggest that you try to use the following types if you don't want to use chlorine solutions (to which some people are quite sensitive): quaternary ammoniums (Roccal, A-33, Endbac) or phenolic disinfectants. Mix solutions at manufacturer's recommended amounts and use as a dip and as a spot cleaner and disinfectant. The ammoniums are quite safe and rapidly break down on contact with organic material. Phenolics also appear to be safe, although they were not used for many years with reptiles because it was thought that they could be toxic (primarily because of the strong odor they give off). Research has shown that, at least with snakes, phenolics are safe and are superior to ammoniums because they have a broader spectrum of activity against herp pathogens (disease-causing organisms). Check with your vet or a veterinary supply store for sources for these disinfectants. Quaternary ammoniums and phenolics should not, however, be used to clean or disinfect amphibian units. These compounds are quite toxic to all manner of amphibians (I speak from experience, having accidentally killed a number of Asian treefrogs many years ago, when I mixed up my water and disinfectant spray bottles. Which reminds me: always label any bottles containing any solution [including water] that you may be using around your herps. Be sure

to read the contents of those bottles before you start spraying willy-nilly. Accidents do happen, as noted.). Alternatively, a mild soap solution may be used for amphibians as long as the unit is thoroughly rinsed (at least twice) and dried. Be sure that you also disinfectant any utensils you use in cleaning and that they are disinfected between different enclosures. Last, and this is very important, disinfect your hands. Your hands are wonderful means of transmitting microscopic parasites and parasite eggs. Clean and disinfect them every time you handle your animals and every time you clean their cages. A good practice is to keep a gallon or so of disinfectant available at all times and soak your cleaning instruments in the solution. Dip your hands as you dip your tools (of course, taking care not to handle specimens with solution-soaked hands). It may not help your skin condition much, but it will do wonders in preventing disease transmission.

**EVALUATING FOODS**
   Another area to watch closely in parasite transmission is the food you give to your captives. Many people feed their insect-eating captives (in particular amphibians and lizards) bugs from outdoors. Although these foods are an excellent source of nutrition, they

**Facing Page:** Perhaps the most important preventive measure a keeper can exercise is routine cleaning of the animals' enclosures. Simple dish soap is adequate for basic cleaning, but a touch of bleach should be added for more thorough cleansing.

are also an excellent source of parasites. To prevent parasite transmission from insects, you must freeze the food for at least ten days. As most amphibians will not accept dead food items, this is a problem. If you feed live, wild insects, be prepared to take your animal to a vet on a regular basis for routine worming. Always try to feed domestically-cultivated foods such as vestigial-winged fruitflies, European gray crickets, and lab mice. Be forewarned, though, that this is not necessarily a guarantee that your animals will not pick up parasites from these foods, especially if the food producers themselves do not practice good husbandry with their feed animals. I have seen repeated cases of pinworm infections in captive herps that I am convinced came from crickets and lab mice,

the latter of which came from less than prime cricket or mouse producers. Lab mice can be a major source of tapeworm infection and the type of tapeworm they transmit can be very nasty. As with many parasites, make sure your food sources are prime and come from clean stock.

## TO TREAT OR NOT TO TREAT

This may seem like a pretty obvious situation. As you will see in some of the following accounts, things may not always be as they appear. Many herp importers assume that new animals coming in are carrying some sort of parasite or parasites and will automatically treat these animals with broad-spectrum parasiticides without conducting specific tests to determine what kind of parasite

Evaluating the livefoods you give to your herptiles will help keep parasitic invasion to a minimum. Make sure the items (like these captive-bred crickets) are well-fed, and further given a healthy dose of vitamin.

W. P. MARA

Rodents are a food item offered to many herptiles. The most common are mice and rats, which can be purchased in quantity through many pet shops. Domestically bred and raised food items are almost always superior to any that have been procured from the wild. You always run the risk of passing on disease when offering wild-caught food items to your pets. Photo of a Timor Monitor, *Varanus timorensis*, eating a rat.

is present and what the degree of parasitism is. Although there is nothing apparently wrong with this practice in high-volume situations, treating prophylactically carries risks. Many of the anti-parasite drugs mentioned herein have various degrees of toxicity, both for the parasite and for the host. These toxins would not be effective in treating parasitic disease if they weren't toxic, would they? These anti-parasitics may have so-called side effects for the animal being treated. Where adverse effects from these drugs are known for herps, I have noted them. However, many herps present in the trade, especially foreign exotics, have little, if any, known veterinary histories and they may react badly to drugs which have been used safely in other herps. This is something you should consider, especially if you have heard that it is alright to begin treating animals with broad-spectrum anti-parasitics without doing specific tests to determine whether or not your animal(s) are hosting some sort of creepy-crawlie. It is not alright and drugs should never be administered without a specific reason. This is one of the reasons why it is so important to consult with your vet. "Shotgun treatments" may do considerably more harm than good and should be avoided.

# DIAGNOSTIC METHODS

This chapter is meant only to give some explanation for the various methods that your veterinarian or vet tech may use to determine what manner of parasite may be residing on or in your pet. This does not mean that you should attempt to conduct these tests yourself. In some countries it is illegal for anyone but a licensed veterinarian to conduct these tests and make diagnoses.

## VISUAL INSPECTION

Visual inspection is the standard method for diagnosing and determining specific kinds of ectoparasites and a few endoparasites. Pets are closely inspected, literally from head to toe, to reveal the presence of mites, ticks, etc. For small parasites, such as lizard or snake mites, a good magnifying lens may be useful in revealing the presence of these creatures. The mouth cavity and trachea (airway) should also be examined. This type of examination may expose such internal parasites as mouth flukes or pentastome worms.

A procedure that is rarely used but which may be warranted for diagnosing pentastomes is laparoscopy. This is a minor surgical procedure in which a small viewing lens mounted on a thin tube is inserted into an animal's body to closely inspect internal organs. As pentastomes frequently live in the mesenteries

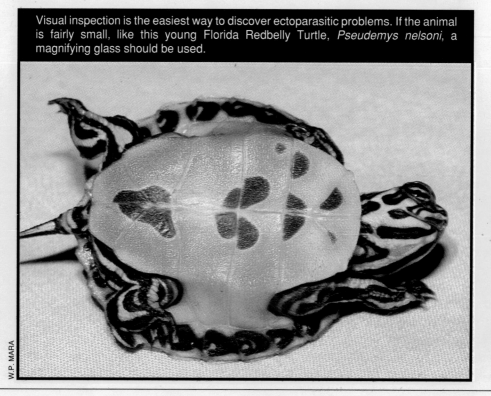

Visual inspection is the easiest way to discover ectoparasitic problems. If the animal is fairly small, like this young Florida Redbelly Turtle, *Pseudemys nelsoni*, a magnifying glass should be used.

W.P. MARA

W. P. MARA

Pay particularly close attention to the head (above—*Eumeces schneideri*) and between the dorsal scales (below—*Crotalus scutulatus*), for these are the places where ectoparasites seem to hide most often. Around and just inside the mouth may also give clues to endoparasitic invasion as well.

W. P. MARA

(tissue which connects internal organs, especially gastrointestinal organs), visualization by endoscope may be one of the few methods through which one can positively demonstrate pentastomiasis.

## MICROSCOPIC INSPECTION

Microscopic techniques are the ones used in the vast majority of cases to demonstrate the presence of internal parasites.

### Blood Smears

A small sample of blood is taken from the subject and spread in a thin film on a microscope slide. The slide is then air-dried for several hours and the blood smear is subjected to certain kinds of stains, depending on what the vet or vet tech is trying to reveal. The stained slide is then examined under a microscope.

This technique reveals parasites such as malaria, trypanosomes, microfilaria, pyroplasms, etc. It may also reveal other abnormalities in the blood or the presence of bacteria.

Blood can be obtained from amphibians and reptiles in the following ways: caecilians—heart puncture; salamanders—caudal vein (the vein on the underside of the tail) puncture or toe clipping (where a small chunk of toe is clipped off); anurans (frogs, toads, and the like)—toe clipping; crocodilians—caudal vein puncture or heart puncture; turtles—toe clipping, toenail drilling (for very large tortoises), caudal vein puncture, or heart puncture; lizards—toe clipping, caudal vein puncture, heart puncture; snakes—caudal vein puncture, heart puncture. Some of these techniques, especially

Blood samples, smeared on a glass slide and then dried, are often the keys to discovering parasites. Shown here is the egg of a *Bothridium* tapeworm taken from a Western Diamondback Rattlesnake, *Crotalus atrox*.

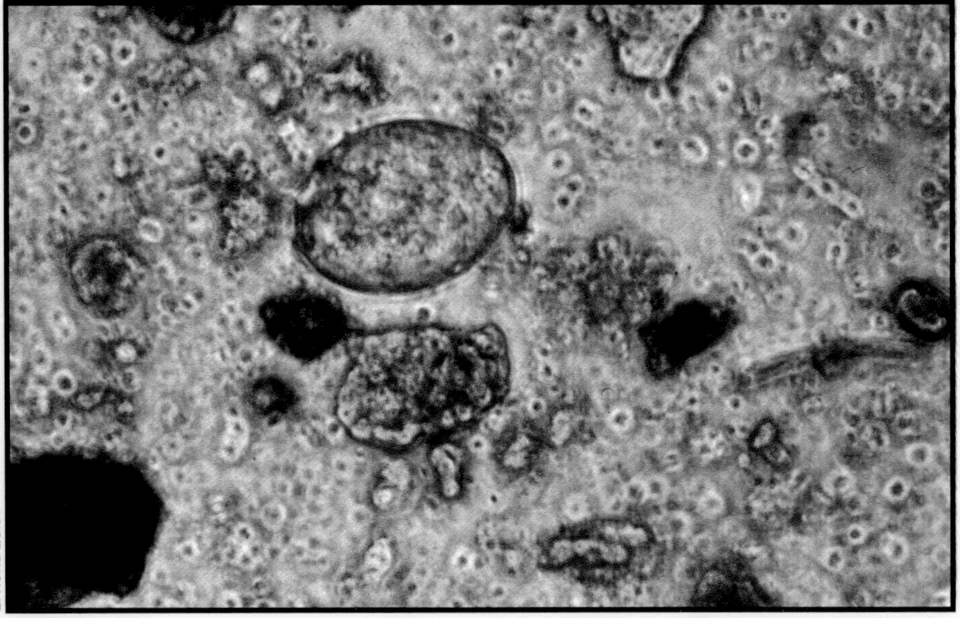

E. RUNDQUIST

E. RUNDQUIST

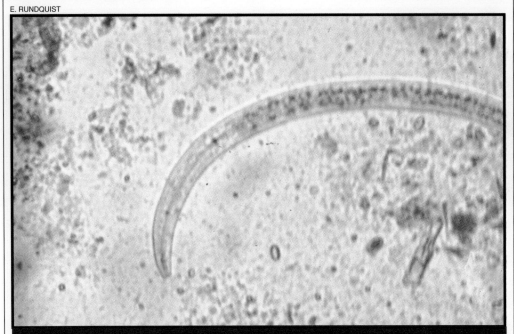

The majority of herptile keepers will not have the facilities required to create usable smears, so the animal(s) will have to be taken to a veterinarian for blood sample collecting. Photo of a nematode from a Dyeing Poison Frog, *Dendrobates tinctorius*.

heart puncture, may sound dangerous, but if performed properly will cause no damage to the pet. Veterinarians who have little experience with herps should consult with a zoo veterinarian who has exotic herp experience for advice as to the proper method by which to conduct these procedures.

### Fecal Examination

Fecal exams are the most commonly practiced diagnostic technique for endoparasites, and there are several different fecal exam techniques. You should present your vet with relatively fresh samples. Material that has dried out is usually unacceptable for fecal tests. Collect a small portion (one to five grams; it is not necessary to give great masses of

this stuff to a vet or vet tech for analysis. They don't like poop any more than you do.) of fecal matter and put it into some sort of sealed container. I have found that 35 mm film canisters are ideal. The material may be stored in the refrigerator for a few days until you are able to take it to your veterinarian. Stored samples over seven days old should be discarded and a fresh sample collected.

The most basic fecal exam is called direct smear examination. A small portion of feces (preferably fresh) is mixed with a small amount of distilled water or saline solution and then a thin smear is spread on a microscope and covered with a cover glass. Welled microscope slides may also be used. The slides are then

DR. FREDRIC L. FRYE IN *REPTILE CARE*

Cryptosporidiosis, which usually can be treated with reasonable expectation of recovery in its early stages by a veterinarian, has caused gastric enlargement in this San Luis Potosi Kingsnake, *Lampropeltis mexicana*.

examined at various powers under a microscope to reveal parasite eggs, larvae, or in rare cases, adults. Direct fecal exams generally only indicate the presence of a parasite and not the actual worm burden. Direct fecal exams are also effective in exposing certain types of parasite eggs that may not float (the next

*Cryptosporidium* sp. are nonhemic protozoans that have been found in the tissues and feces of many herptiles. Many protozoans can be found in clinically normal herptiles, only becoming pathogenic when an animal becomes highly stressed or immunologically inept.

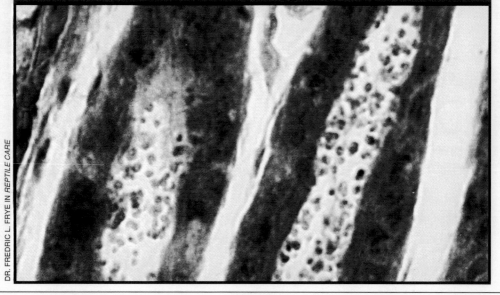

DR. FREDRIC L. FRYE IN *REPTILE CARE*

DR. FREDRIC L. FRYE IN REPTILE CARE

A further example of gastric enlargement due to cryptosporidiosis, in this case in an American Rat Snake, *Elaphe obsoleta*.

procedure discussed). These eggs include flukes, acanthocephalans, and certain tapeworms. However, direct fecal exams are the only ones that will reveal protozoan parasites such as flagellates, ciliates, and amoebas.

Fecal flotation examination should always be done in conjunction with direct smear exams. Again, a small portion of fresh feces (a gram or less) is mixed with a chemical solution that has a higher specific gravity than certain parasite eggs. In layman's terms, this means that the eggs will float rather than sink to the bottom of the solution. Common fecal flotation solutions are zinc sulfate, magnesium sulfate, or sugar solutions. Once the fecal mixture has been made,

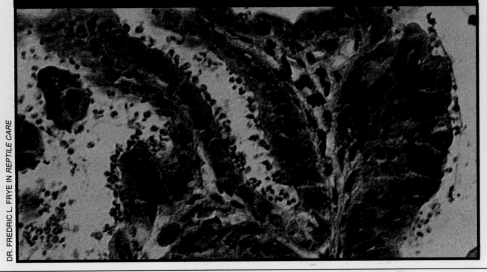

This histologic section of gastric mucosa shows a heavy infestation of minute *Cryptosporidium* sp. Due to the alarmingly high number of recent cases of cryptosporidiosis in snakes and lizards, many researchers believe the problem to be as common as invasion of the well-known *Entamoeba invadens*, and furthermore just as effective for the wiping out of entire animal collections.

DR. FREDRIC L. FRYE IN REPTILE CARE

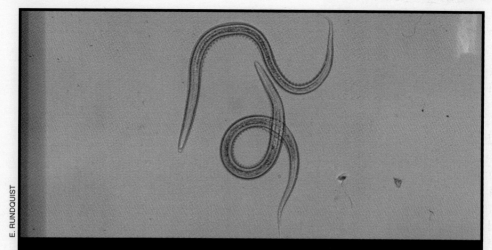

E. RUNDQUIST

Hookworm larvae from a Boa Constrictor, *Boa constrictor*. Some of the major signs of hookworm infestation include anemia, weight loss, and lack of appetite.

a tube of some sort is filled to the top with this solution and a slide cover glass is placed on top of the tube and in contact with the fecal solution. After a short period (about five minutes), the cover glass is carefully removed and placed on a microscope slide. The slide is then examined as for direct smears. Fecal flotations will reveal eggs and larvae of virtually all nematodes (so-called roundworms), pentastomes, gut mites, many tapeworms, coccidia, and cryptosporidians. Fecal flotations also give a vet or vet tech a pretty good idea as to the particular worm burden (the numbers of parasites present) of an infected animal, as all eggs and larvae should float to the surface of the flotation solution and adhere to the cover glass. Fecal flotations will not reveal the intestinal protozoans previously mentioned, as the solution kills and destroys the parasites.

Sedimentation examination is similar to direct fecal exams. This method is particularly effective in diagnosing the presence and numbers of flukes. A one-gram sample of feces is mixed with distilled water or saline solution. This mixture is then poured through a filter that removes the larger particles in the solution. This procedure is then repeated. A test tube is filled with the filtered solution and put into a centrifuge for several minutes at low power. After centrifugation, the clear solution is poured off and a portion of the remaining solid pellet is mixed again with a small portion of distilled water or saline solution. A drop of this mixture is placed onto a microscope slide and covered with a cover glass. This slide is then checked under a microscope for parasite eggs.

Baermann sedimentation is the final technique I will cover here. It is not often used to diagnose parasites but I have found it highly effective in assessing the type and degree of certain parasite infections. First, the

Baermann apparatus (named for the inventor of the device and technique) is set up. This apparatus basically looks like a funnel set in a clamp holder and having a rubber tube with a clamp attached to the outlet of the funnel. Coarse filter material, such as cheesecloth or gauze padding, is placed in the funnel and the funnel is filled with distilled water, after making sure that the tube clamp is secured tightly. Fecal material is then placed in the funnel on top of the filter material and this "solution" is left to sit for at least 12 (and up to 24) hours. After the settling period, approximately one milliliter of the solution is decanted from the device after loosening the clamp. A small amount of this solution is then placed on a microscope slide, covered with a cover slip, and examined under a microscope. Well slides may also be used and are particularly good for observing live larvae. What happens is this: as many worm larvae are positively geotropic (which is scientificese for attempting to burrow), as they burrow through the feces and past the filter, they gradually descend through the water column to where the rubber tube is clamped. Many eggs will descend here also. As larval identification can be important in determining the exact type of worm present, Baermann sedimentation can be an important diagnostic tool. This technique is most effective when culturing worm eggs, especially hookworms or *Capillaria*. It will also give the vet or vet tech a good idea of your pet's worm burden. I have found some incredible worm infections, especially strongyles, after making use of the Baermann sedimentation technique.

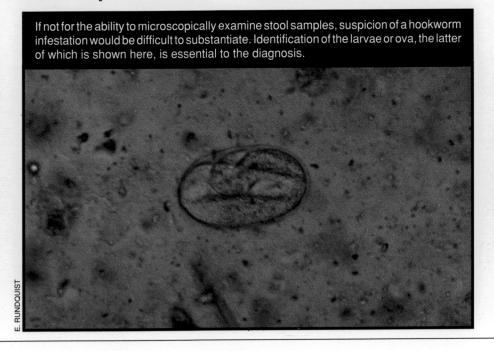

If not for the ability to microscopically examine stool samples, suspicion of a hookworm infestation would be difficult to substantiate. Identification of the larvae or ova, the latter of which is shown here, is essential to the diagnosis.

E. RUNDQUIST

# ECTOPARASITES

### AMPHIBIAN MITES

Mites are perhaps the most commonly observed parasites of amphibians and reptiles. In amphibians, it isn't obvious whether or not they cause significant problems and they cause fewer problems in reptiles than generally believed. However, they are a bother.

Amphibian mites are usually found on aquatic or semi-aquatic frogs and toads and smooth, moist-skinned salamanders. These mites are called trombiculids. I doubt that they cause serious illness in most amphibians but that have been associated with the loss of fingers and toes in certain salamanders.

### Diagnosis

In frogs and toads—red bumps on the belly and underside of arms and legs. Do not confuse this condition with the serious bacterial illness in frogs called red-leg. Trombiculid mites cause a small but definite swelling for each mite. In red-leg, the area is usually not raised and, if you look closely, the reddish area is actually a small hemorrhage (bleeding under the skin). The red area in mite infestations is the actual mite.

In salamanders—on light areas, a reddish bump as in frogs. On darker skin, you may need a small hand lens to see the reddish mite under the dark skin. Mites are usually found on fingers, toes, hands, and feet. The may occasionally occur on legs and the belly.

### Treatment

Frogs and toads—soak your

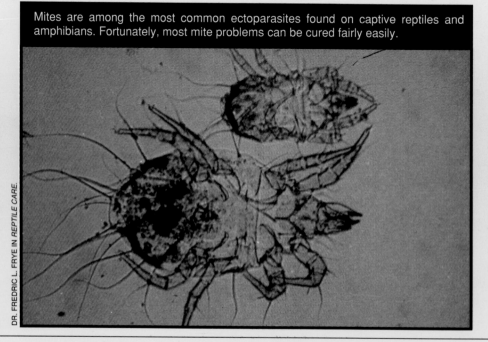

Mites are among the most common ectoparasites found on captive reptiles and amphibians. Fortunately, most mite problems can be cured fairly easily.

DR. FREDRIC L. FRYE IN *REPTILE CARE*.

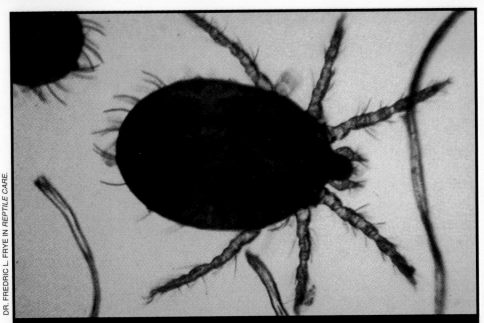

In the juvenile stage of some parasitic mites, specimens will have only three pairs of legs. As adults, many of these will have a fourth pair, sprouting posteriorly.

DR. FREDRIC L. FRYE IN *REPTILE CARE.*

animals in a bath of tetracycline solution (such as Polyotic) overnight. The exact dosage of tetracycline is not absolutely critical. If your vet is using Polyotic, the solution should be about the color of light lager beer. Discard this solution after 48 hours as it degrades rapidly. Repeat treatments may be necessary.

Salamanders—since salamanders as a rule do not tolerate soaking in chemical solutions, you will have to remove the mites manually. That means getting very fine-pointed forceps and digging the little buggers out. For large, common salamanders this procedure usually causes no problems. With small or very rare salamanders, the stress of handling may kill the specimen. It is best with these animals to remove only two or three mites at a time to reduce stress. You may choose not to remove the mites at all. I have observed mites disappearing without treatment on a number of salamanders over time.

## LIZARD MITES

True lizard mites are usually found on rough-scaled species such American fence lizards (*Sceloporus*), Old World agamids (family Chamaeleonidae), and other species like American collared lizards (*Crotaphytus*). In fact, it appears that certain species of lizards have evolved "mite pockets" at front limb insertions expressly for the purpose of supporting these mites. This indicates that there is some sort of commensal relationship between the mites

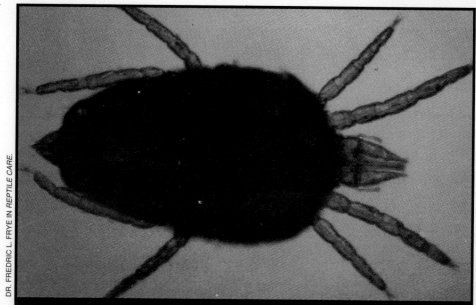

DR. FREDRIC L. FRYE IN *REPTILE CARE.*

Shown is a mite species known as *Hirstiella trombiidiformes*, characterized by the point at the end of the abdomen. This specimen was taken from a Chuckwalla, *Sauromalus obesus*.

and the lizards. I am not aware of any specific problems that lizards mites may cause in captives and would choose for myself not to treat them. If you do so, the following treatment should work.

**Diagnosis**

Lizard mites are invariably found at and behind the point where the front limbs meet the body and generally look like a patch of orange or red bumps. Closer examination with a hand lens will reveal the mites.

**Treatment**

Lightly spray the animal with a 1% solution of Permectrin (a synthetic pyrethrin-type insecticide which is very safe to use with animals), toweling the animal off immediately afterward and taking care to avoid spraying the head. Separate the animal in a well-ventilated holding unit for at least 24 hours, neither feeding nor watering it during this period.

**SNAKE MITES**

Snake mites almost invariably invoke panic among some herp keepers. This is because, at one time, these parasites were thought to be a vector for a highly pathogenic blood disease. More recent research shows that mites are probably not carriers for this disease, but this doesn't mean you should ignore the presence of mites in your collection. Snake mites are a very good indicator that your basic husbandry isn't up to what it should be. Dirty units are wonderful breeding grounds for these pests. Even under the best husbandry, snake mites sometimes show up in a collection. Fortunately, they are fairly easily controlled.

On occasion, your vet or vet technician may come across mite eggs while doing a fecal examination. These eggs almost invariably come from either mouse mites or what are called gut mites. Neither type of mite causes problems and are no cause for concern or treatment.

### Diagnosis

True snake mites can occur on any snake and occasionally maybe found on lizards such as skinks. They appear to be black or dark brown blobs, about 0.5 mm/0.02 in in diameter, that move about the animal's skin. They are particularly prevalent around the head and eyes or ear openings (in lizards). In heavy infestations, your animal may appear to have been dusted with flour.

### Treatment

Remove the infected animal(s) to a sterile holding unit. Spray the animal lightly with a 1% Permectrin solution (again, avoiding the mouth) and wipe off any excess solution. Keep the animal in the holding unit for 24 hours, without food or water. Next, completely clean out the infected animal's cage and throw away any substrate or cage props such as wood or rocks. Disinfect the unit thoroughly, clean with hot, soapy water, rinse with hot water, and then allow the unit to dry for at least 24 hours before setting it up with new substrate and cage props. Be sure the animal's water bowl is also thoroughly disinfected and cleaned.

Repeat treatments may be necessary, as Permectrin does not

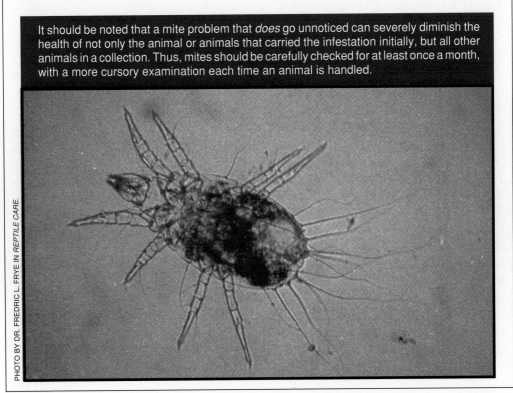

It should be noted that a mite problem that *does* go unnoticed can severely diminish the health of not only the animal or animals that carried the infestation initially, but all other animals in a collection. Thus, mites should be carefully checked for at least once a month, with a more cursory examination each time an animal is handled.

PHOTO BY DR. FREDRIC L. FRYE IN *REPTILE CARE*.

affect mite eggs that may have been laid on the specimen's body.

CAUTION: Although I have used Permectrin for years without any observed adverse affects, I have recently heard of a couple of cases of possible poisoning in a lizard and a snake. It appears in both cases that the affected animals drank some of the treatment solution, so it is important that you do not allow your pets to soak in the solution or drink it while applying. If you follow the above protocol rigorously, you shouldn't have any problem. Another treatment is ivermectin at 200 micrograms (mcg) per kilogram (kg) body weight given as a subcutaneous (SQ) injection once. This will kill adult mites feeding on your snake. A solution of ivermectin may also be used to lightly spray the animal and then lightly wiping the animal down. Spray the same solution into the animal's cleaned and disinfected cage. This should take care of any mite nymphs that hatch from the microscopic eggs in the days to come. Using an ivermectin injection has however, proven fatal to some turtles, so its use should be carefully monitored.

Some herpetoculturists have reported using Sevin dust (5% or 7%) to successfully treat snake and lizard mites. The regime reported for using this insecticide is as follows: sprinkle Sevin on a towel laid on a flat surface. Lay your snake on the towel, grasp the snake behind the head with the dusted towel, and then allow the animal to crawl completely through the towel. Put the snake in a clean unit for 24 hours, then wipe off the Sevin dust and any mites (which should be dead) with a moist paper towel and discard the towel. A second Sevin treatment 48 hours later is also recommended. I have no experience with this particular treatment and you should consult with your veterinarian before attempting it. It also seems that additional treatment one to two weeks later may be necessary, as mite eggs begin to hatch.

## TICKS

Ticks may be found on turtles, lizards, and snakes. Although they do not appear to cause major problems, they indicate that your animal just came out of the wild recently. Anyone who tries to sell you an animal with ticks and says it is a long-term captive or captive-bred doesn't know what they are talking about. Be forewarned. Animals with ticks should also be checked for internal parasites.

### Diagnosis

Reptile ticks look like any other kind of tick, except they are usually smaller. Your vet will be able to confirm their identity if you are unsure of what they are.

### Treatment

Remove with forceps, making sure to grasp the tick at its mouth parts and pulling gently (don't just yank them out). After removal, treat the bite area with a topical antibiotic such as Panalog, Neosporin, or any one of the many "triple antibiotic" gels, until the wound heals.

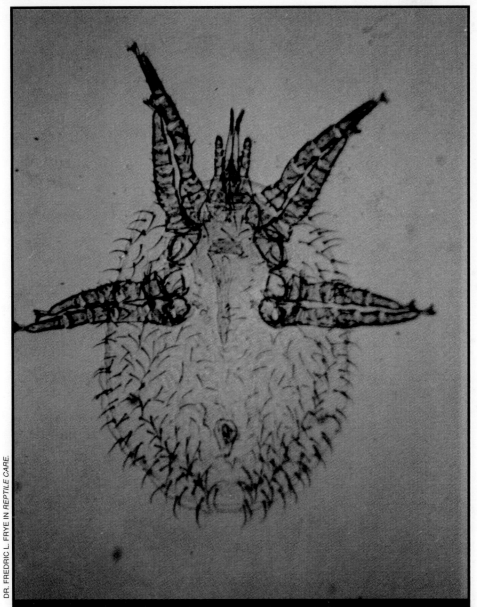

DR. FREDRIC L. FRYE IN *REPTILE CARE*.

Shown is a cleared example of the common snake mite *Ophionyssus natricis*. A fairly gentle way to eradicate a mild mite infestation is to bathe the patient, or patients, in warm water for about four to five hours daily, for a period of about one week.

## LEECHES

Leeches are usually found on aquatic turtles. They may also affect certain aquatic amphibians. Heavy infestations may cause anemia and some leeches may transmit other parasites.

### Diagnosis

Again, herp leeches look like any other kind of leech. Your vet can confirm their identity. In turtles, they are usually found where the front and/or hind limbs meet the body. They be dark gray or brown and there are usually several at one site.

**Treatment**
Treatment is as for ticks.

**FLY LARVAE**
Fly larvae are found on terrestrial turtles and particularly affect American box turtles (*Terrapene*). Any turtle that is keep outside in warmer months may be affected. These larvae generally do not cause serious illness, but the wounds they create may be a source of bacterial infection.

**Diagnosis**
Consult your vet. Initial indications may be a swelling under the skin with a small, open wound that is leaking fluid. These lesions are usually found near the front or hind limbs. If the wound opening is retracted slightly, you should be able to see a pale maggot inside. It may withdraw deeper into the wound when exposed.

**Treatment**
The maggot may be removed with a hooked needle or fine forceps, taking care not to rip it open or otherwise spread its innards in the wound. Application of a light anesthetic cream may immobilize the maggot. After removal, thoroughly flush the lesion with saline solution or lactated Ringer's solution and then liberally inject a topical antibiotic such as Panalog, Neocin, or Polysporin. Treat the wound daily until it heals.

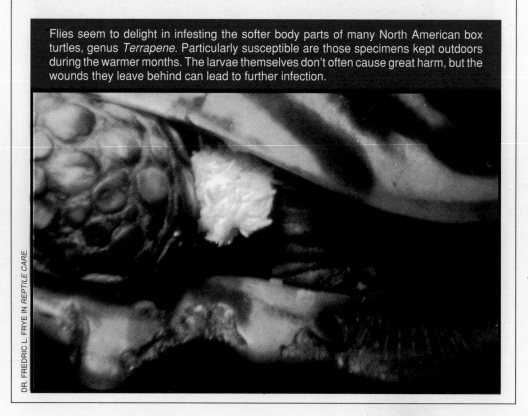

Flies seem to delight in infesting the softer body parts of many North American box turtles, genus *Terrapene*. Particularly susceptible are those specimens kept outdoors during the warmer months. The larvae themselves don't often cause great harm, but the wounds they leave behind can lead to further infection.

DR. FREDRIC L. FRYE IN *REPTILE CARE.*

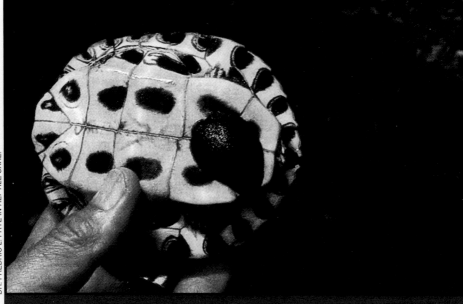

DR. FREDRIC L. FRYE IN *REPTILE CARE.*

**Above:** A rather large leech attached to the belly of a Red-eared Slider, *Trachemys scripta elegans*. **Below:** Leeches can appear as tiny little squiggles, or very large, almost horrifying creatures that sometimes lurk around an aquatic turtle's tank in search of a host, as this *Placobdella* sp. is doing.

DR. FREDRIC L. FRYE IN *REPTILE CARE.*

# ENDOPARASITES

Endoparasites are the major disease-causing parasites of herps and some of them can be quite devastating. I'll start this section with protozoans (single-celled organisms) and go to worms.

## MALARIAL PARASITES

Most people don't think about their animals as having malaria. There are a surprising number of kinds of malarial organisms that occur in amphibians and reptiles, particularly smaller lizards. Whether or not they cause disease in herps is problematic but they have been associated with Paget's Disease (a bone disease) in snakes and almost certainly reduce the life span of any affected animal. Malarias are not directly transmissible to other animals, as they require a mosquito host.

### Diagnosis

Malaria can only be diagnosed by a veterinary technician or vet, by examining specially stained slides of blood. There are usually no apparent direct symptoms in affected animals. Swelling of vertebral bone in snakes may be an indicator, but this must be confirmed via radiograph (X-ray photos). Affected animals may also be listless and eat irregularly.

### Treatment

I am not aware of any particular treatment for herp malarias. The human anti-malarial drugs chloroquin, amodaquin, and primaquin may be useful, but they are toxic and any treatment would be experimental. Your vet may offer other options. Some workers have suggested maintaining reptiles at high temperatures (90 to 94°F/32 to 35°C) for 24 hours. If you choose to try this, be sure that your pet can withstand such high temperatures. Many reptiles cannot and I doubt that any amphibian could.

## MICROFILARIA

Microfilaria are very small worms (hence the name micro-) which are usually found in an animal's blood system. Heartworms of dogs are a good example. The incidence of this type of parasite in captive herps is largely unknown but they do occur in wild reptiles, particularly Asian snakes. Pythons from New Guinea may be particularly susceptible. As these worms require an intermediate host (mosquito, fly), they are not transmissible from one specimen to another. Although the pathogenicity of microfilaria are again largely unknown, wild-caught snakes from Asia and the Indo-Australian region should be checked. In fact, any herp from the tropics would merit testing.

### Diagnosis

Positive diagnosis is made from stained blood smear examination. Animals infected with these worms may show chronic wasting, even if they feed regularly. There are usually no other signs.

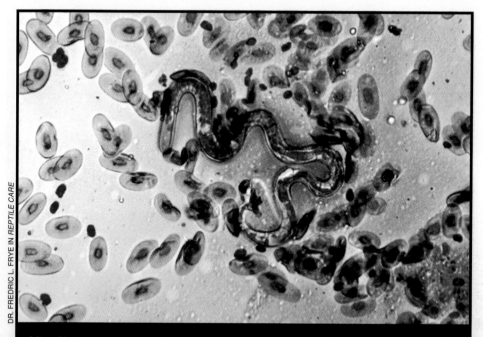

DR. FREDRIC L. FRYE IN *REPTILE CARE*

Microfilaria are not generally believed to be common in herptiles, but have been found in a few wild snakes, particularly those from Asia. Detecting their presence is done with a stained blood smear, and they usually aren't difficult to deal with once discovered. **Above,** a microfilaria worm from a Trans-Pecos Rat Snake, *Bogertophis subocularis*. **Below,** the same from a Madagascan chameleon.

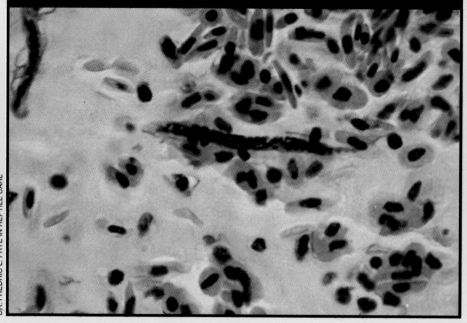

DR. FREDRIC L. FRYE IN *REPTILE CARE*

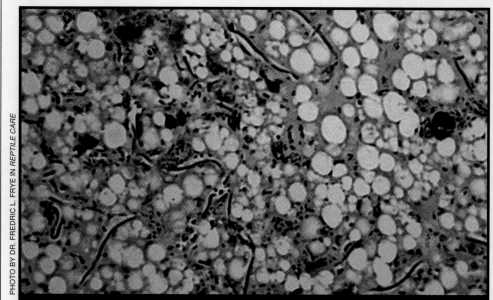

PHOTO BY DR. FREDRIC L. FRYE IN *REPTILE CARE*

Often it is not the presence of microfilaria that causes an animal's demise, but toxic shock from the treatment to have them eradicated. Heavy infestation calls for heavy treatment, and the longer the problem goes unnoticed, the lesser the chances of recovery.

**Treatment**

Ivermectin at 200 mcg/kg given IM once should be effective. There may be drawbacks to this treatment, though. Animals with a heavy worm load may die from toxic shock after treatment. I am aware of just such a case in a Boelen's Python (*Python boeleni*), a rare, very expensive and spectacular snake from New Guinea. In this case, even though the specimen was known to have a heavy infestation of microfilaria, the decision was made to treat because of the animal's rarity and because it was felt by the owners that the worm infection would probably kill the snake anyway. When one is dealing with wild-caught exotic herps, cure or kill is many times the only viable treatment option. You should work closely with your vet in deciding on whether or not to treat any animal with a microfilaria infection.

**COCCIDIA**

Coccidia are peculiar little beasts that live in the lining of your animal's gut. They can occur in just about any type of amphibian or reptile and they are fairly transmissible. They can be highly pathogenic.

**Diagnosis**

Rapid weight loss, bloody or blood-tinged, somewhat loose stools. Confirmation is by direct fecal examination or fecal flotation examination by a vet tech or vet.

**Treatment**

Corid at 10 mg/kg given orally one time a day for six days is effective. In addition, tribrissen at 30 mg/kg body weight given IM once daily for six days also works.

BOTH PHOTOS BY DR. FREDRIC L. FRYE IN *REPTILE CARE*

Coccidia are a group (subclass) of protozoans that usually inhabit the epithelial tissues (those that line cavities and ducts) where they will cause rapid weight loss and bloody stools. They are highly pathogenic and are known to pass from one animal to another. **Above**, the sporulated oocyst (*Isospora* sp.) from a Reticulated Python, *Python reticulatus*. **Below**, a group of sporulated oocysts (*Eimeria* sp.) from a Burmese Python.

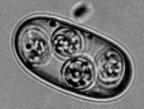

Cases that fail to respond to these treatments may respond to metronidazole (Flagyl, Flagenase) at 50 to 125 mg/kg body weight give once orally and once again seven days later. After treatment, schedule regular fecal exams every three months for one year. The coccidial organism isn't shed regularly into fecal matter and it may not be detected without these regular exams.

## CRYPTOSPORIDIOSIS

Crypto is a relatively newly recognized disease in herps, and has been linked with serious illness in many reptiles, particularly snakes. It is caused by a very small coccidian which is difficult to detect. You may have heard about crypto being linked with illness in humans. It can be present in drinking water and causes a flu-like illness. It has also been associated with serious illness in AIDS patients. Let me stress that even though your animals may have crypto, there is no evidence that reptilian crypto can be transmitted to humans. Crypto may be highly transmissible to other herps, however.

### Diagnosis

Chronic regurgitation within a few days after eating, chronic wasting, death. The organism is confirmed by direct smear fecal examination. If you suspect crypto, be sure to have your vet or vet tech do a specific test for the organism. Because of its small size, it is frequently missed in routine fecal exams.

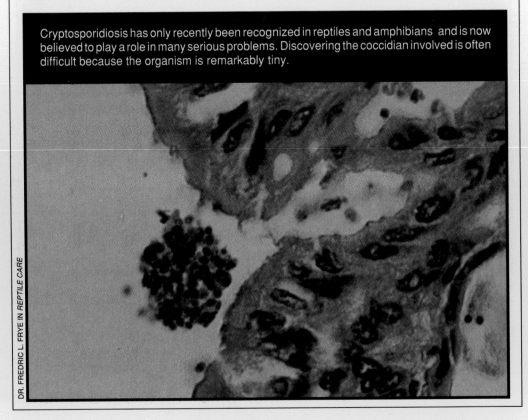

Cryptosporidiosis has only recently been recognized in reptiles and amphibians and is now believed to play a role in many serious problems. Discovering the coccidian involved is often difficult because the organism is remarkably tiny.

DR. FREDRIC L. FRYE IN REPTILE CARE

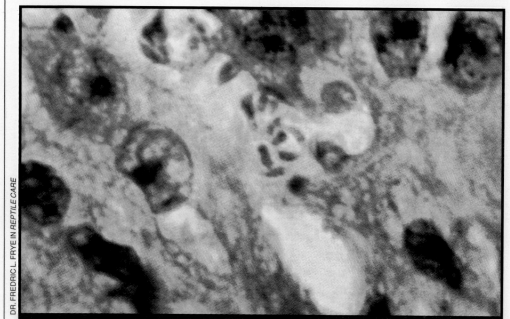

DR. FREDRIC L. FRYE IN *REPTILE CARE*

"Crypto" (a somewhat slangish nickname for cryptosporidiosis) has been loosely connected with a number of human illnesses as well as those in herptiles, but it is important to note that there is presently no evidence to suggest that a herptile with crypto can pass it on to its keeper.

**Treatment**

This is a bad one, I'm afraid. At this time, there is no known treatment for herp cryptosporidosis. One worker has claimed success with trimethoprim sulfa (dosage unknown) but I am unaware of anyone else having any success with drug treatment. Others have suggested feeding small amounts of food (1/4 to 1/2 normal) every five days or so, and this may have some promise. Although this method does not eliminate the parasite, it may allow the host time to build a natural immunity, if the specimen is not too wasted. However, the prospects for the long run are not good. You should immediately separate your infected animal from all others and then begin fecal checks on every animal in your collection. You may have to run these checks for several months, as the organism is not constantly passed in fecal material. What you do with your infected animal(s) is up to you and it is a difficult decision. My personal inclination would be to euthanize the creature, as it will always remain a potential source of infection. You may choose to try the above treatments but if the animal fails to respond, the humane thing to do is to euthanize it. Do not release the animal and do not pass it along to someone else.

**INTESTINAL FLAGELLATES**

Flagellates are very common parasites of amphibians and reptiles and their ability to cause disease has caused some debate.

However, I believe (as do many others) that trichomonad flagellates can cause serious disease and should be treated upon discovery. There is one possible exception to that. Aquatic turtles (such as sliders, genus *Trachemys*) do not appear to be affected by trichomonads and you may choose not to treat them. However, if you have other herps in your collection, these infected turtles will be a potential source of infection. There are a number of other kinds of flagellated organisms that I have observed in herps (such as *Hexamita*) and I do not know whether these beasties can cause disease. It is probably best to treat for them also.

**Diagnosis**

Rapid weight loss, loose watery stools (particularly evident on paper substrates) occasionally with traces of blood, regurgitation. The animal will frequently have a normal appetite. Diagnosis is made by direct fecal examination by a vet tech or vet. Stools should be presented for examination as soon as possible after they have been passed, as most flagellates dissolve rapidly after leaving the gut. Try to get a stool for examination within four hours after it has been passed or refrigerate the stool and get it to a vet within 10 hours.

**Treatment**

The drug of choice is metronidazole at 50 to 125 mg/kg body weight. Emetine hydrochloride at 106 mg/kg has also been used successfully. These drugs should be given once orally (or injected into a food

Interestingly, slider turtles, genus *Trachemys*, do not seem to be affected by trichomonad flagellates, although there is some debate over just how pathogenic some flagellates seem to be. Photo of a Yellowbelly Slider, *Trachemys scripta scripta*.

W. P. MARA

W. P. MARA

There are strong arguments in favor of the theory that aquatic turtles pose the greatest threat to a keeper in regards to the carrying and possible transmitting of parasites. They are certainly among the filthiest of captive herptiles and thus require a great amount of attention to cleanliness. Photo of a Red-eared Slider, *Trachemys scripta elegans*.

item). Give a follow-up treatment one week later and submit additional stools for examination to determine if the parasite has been eliminated.

## AMOEBAS

This is another bad news beast. Amoebas can be highly pathogenic and are highly transmissible. They can quicklydevastate a collection. They are usually found in reptiles but may also occur in amphibians. Animals that test positive for amoebas should be separated immediately from the rest of the collection. Test the other animals in your collection for this parasite.

### Diagnosis

Your animal will be listless and may refuse to eat. It will show some weight loss, may vomit, and the stools may be loose, foul-smelling, and highly mucoid (whitish, do not confuse with uric acid, which is usually a discrete white or yellow mass). Positive diagnosis is made by direct fecal smear examination.

### Treatment

Metronidazole and emetine hydrochloride as for flagellates are effective. In addition, iodochlorhydrozin and dephenoxylate hydrochloride have been used successfully. The dosage for the former is 0.3 g per kg body weight and for the latter is 1.25 mg per kg, both given once orally. Follow-up fecal exams should be done two to three weeks post-treatment. In addition, maintaining your animal at fairly high temperatures (90°F/32°C) for 24 hours in a low humidity environment may be helpful.

## CILIATES

Ciliates are common intestinal parasites in salamanders, frogs, toads, and turtles. They may also occur in other herps. As the vast majority of ciliates do not cause problems in captive herps, I mention them here primarily because they are common, big, and very active, qualities that may get your vet or vet tech very excited and prone to treat for something that is not pathogenic. There is one exception. The ciliate *Balantidium* may occasionally be found in herps and it can cause problems, both for the animal and for you. *Balantidium* can cause a nasty intestinal upset in people and doesn't appear to be very host specific. If your herp has *Balantidium* you should take precautions to be extra clean. Wash your hands and disinfect your cleaning tools and cages very thoroughly. Separate *Balantidium*-positive specimens immediately.

### Diagnosis

Ciliates are confirmed by direct fecal smear examination. *Balantidium* may cause diarrhea in your captives.

### Treatment

Treatment for *Balantidium* is metronidazole at 50 to 125 mg per kg body weight given once orally is an effective treatment. A follow-up treatment should be given one week later and post-treatment follow-up fecal exams should be conducted 7 to 10 days after the last treatment.

## WORMS

Worms are the other major source of herp parasite disease and there is a bewildering variety of these critters. Herps are prime hosts for an array of larval, intermediate, and adult worms and it is rare to find a wild-caught pet without a worm or two in its belly. Certain kinds of worms can also be common in captive-bred animals. The following section will cover the major worm parasites of herps (nematodes, tapeworms, flukes, acanthocephalans, and pentastomes).

## NEMATODES

Nematodes, or roundworms, are the major worm offenders in the herp world. In this section, I will cover ascarids, strongyles (including *Strongyloides*), hookworms, pinworms (oxyurids), lungworms (*Rhabdias*), whipworms (trichurids), spirurids, and *Capillaria*. All of these worms cause disease of varying degrees of pathogenicity.

### Ascarids

Ascarids are the type of nematode you may have run across in a biology class, those white, 8 to 10 inch worms that usually come from horses. The ascarids in herps are obviously much smaller and, fortunately,

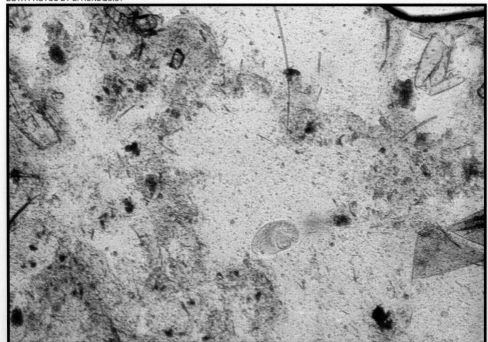

Ciliates are common in herptiles, most commonly in turtles and amphibians, but one genus, *Balantidium*, can cause problems not only in herps but in humans as well. If you find one of your animals to harbor this parasite, give extra attention to cleaning both the implements and yourself. **Above**: A ciliate from a Dyeing Poison Frog, *Dendrobates tinctorius*. **Below**: The same from a Burmese Mountain Tortoise, *Manouria emys*.

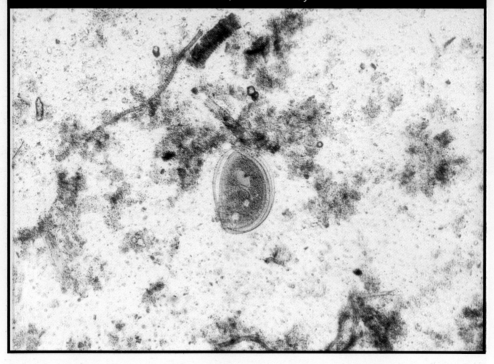

are rather rare. Their ability to cause disease in herps is largely unknown but they have a direct life cycle and should be assumed to be pathogenic. Ascarids should be treated accordingly. The only herps in which I have observed these worms are snake-eating snakes such as kraits (*Bungarus* spp.), the King Cobras (*Ophiophagus hannah*), and Indigo Snakes (*Drymarchon corais*). They should be able to occur, though, in just about any kind of reptile.

### Diagnosis

Adult ascarids may occasionally be passed in feces and will look like pale white, thin worms. Your animal may also vomit masses of them, if they reside in the stomach. These worms should be taken to your vet for identification (this also applies to all worms you might find in fecal matter or vomitus). Larvae and eggs can be confirmed by direct fecal smear exam or fecal floatation.

### Treatment

The treatments of choice are mebendazole or ivermectin. The regime for the former drug is 25 mg per kg body weight given once orally with a follow-up treatment one week later. This drug should not be given to amphibians. Ivermectin, for reptiles, should be given by injection SQ once at 200 mcg per kg (note that the dosage is micrograms, not milligrams). Ivermectin should not be administered to turtles, as it has been linked with a number of fatalities.

If your froggie turns up with ascarids (which is unlikely, but they have been found in salamanders), a new treatment is ivermectin at 2 mg (not

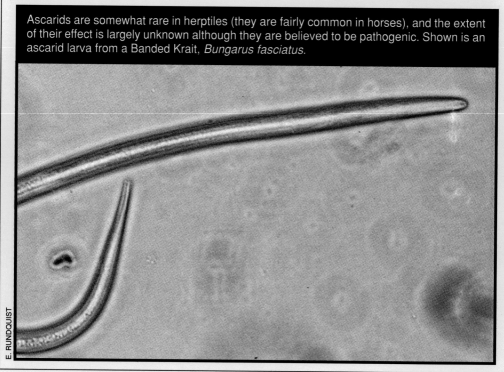

Ascarids are somewhat rare in herptiles (they are fairly common in horses), and the extent of their effect is largely unknown although they are believed to be pathogenic. Shown is an ascarid larva from a Banded Krait, *Bungarus fasciatus.*

E. RUNDQUIST

E. RUNDQUIST

Strongyles are common to herps and can be found in both reptiles and amphibians. They are pathogenic and can multiply to huge numbers, but some animals, particularly herbivorous lizards, may actually benefit as the host of a strongyle colony. Shown is a strongyle from a Gray-banded Kingsnake, *Lampropeltis alterna*.

micrograms here) per kg body weight, applied to the animal's back, once. This treatment has been found to be 100% effective in frogs for other worms.

Follow-up fecal examinations should be done two weeks post-treatment.

## STRONGYLES

Strongyles are the worms most commonly observed in herps and can occur in any species of amphibian or reptile. Their pathogenicity is generally related to numbers of worms in the gut (commonly called a worm load or worm burden) but a relative few can cause problems in small animals. They also have a direct life cycle, which means that they are passed from host to host, or can reinfect a host, by ingesting

eggs or larvae. Cleanliness is a critical factor in keeping these worms at bay.

Certain herbivorous or mostly herbivorous lizards such as ground iguanas (*Cyclura*), Chuckwallas (*Sauromalus obesus*), and Old World mastigures (*Uromastyx*) may have tremendous worm burdens. The numbers present on fecal examination may be astounding and will send any reasonable vet scurrying to the drug cabinet immediately. This is a case where treatment may not necessarily be advisable, as there is evidence that these worms may actually help in digesting the rough plant diet of these animals. If you keep your animals outside year-round and under ideal conditions (whatever those may be), you may not want to treat these lizards for strongyles unless the specimen exhibits overt symptoms of intestinal disease (diarrhea, bloody stools, moderate weight loss, regurgitation). On the other hand, since your maintenance

**Diagnosis**

Captives may show moderate weight loss or be unable to gain weight. Diagnosis is by direct fecal smear examination or fecal flotation (which gives a better idea of the host's worm load).

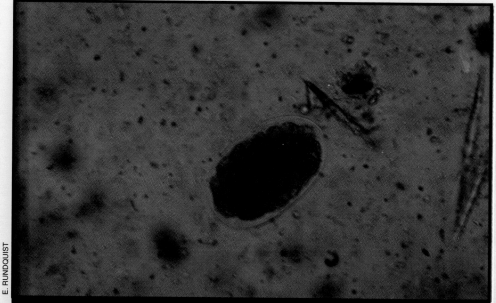

E. RUNDQUIST

Hookworms are not only common in herptiles, but can cause major problems if left untreated. They are particularly common in turtles kept outside. Photo of hookworm ova from a Boa Constrictor, *Boa constrictor*.

conditions may be less than ideal (which is probably no fault of your own. This just reflects the fact that herpetoculture is still somewhat in its infancy and we don't have great understanding of proper maintenance parameters for most species), it probably isn't a bad idea to treat if strongyles are confirmed in your pet. After treatment, be sure to provide your captives with a high-quality diet at about 25% more quantity than usual for at least a month. This should compensate for the lack of those little worm digestors that used to be in your lizard's gut.

**Treatment**

The initial drug of choice is thiabendazole (TBZ) given orally once at 100 mg per kg body weight, with a follow-up treatment in 7 to 10 days. TBZ is one of the safest and most widely used anti-worm drugs because it eliminates worms by irritating them and causing them to be passed in feces. It is the drug of choice for amphibians because of its low toxicity.

Ivermectin and mebendazole at the previously suggested dosages and regimes are also effective against strongyles. For turtles, levamisol phosphate at 8 mg per kg is suggested because it is given by injection and is not as toxic as ivermectin. It should be given once intramuscularly (IM), with a follow-up treatment one week later.

Follow-up fecals should be done post-treatment and reoccurring infections should be treated accordingly.

**Diagnosis**

In snakes, the animal will either show moderate weight loss or will be unable to gain weight. Stools may be rather gooey and gray or tarry in appearance. The specimen may regurgitate occasionally. Symptoms in turtles, lizards, and amphibians are not always present and positive diagnosis for all cases is made by

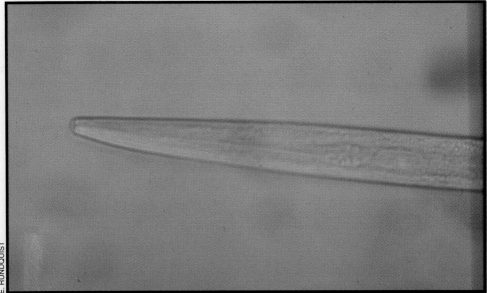

E. RUNDQUIST

Some of the signs of a hookworm invasion include weight loss or the inability to put on weight, grayish stools, and occasional regurgitation, but for a more positive diagnosis a fecal flotation exam must be performed. Photo of a hookworm larva from a Leopard Tortoise, *Geochelone pardalis*.

## HOOKWORMS

Hookworms are another common parasite of herps, usually being found in reptiles. They can be especially common in turtles kept outside, particularly in central and southeastern regions of the U.S. Hooks can cause serious illness and should always be treated for when diagnosed. Their life cycle is direct and infected animals may infect other specimens.

fecal flotation exam. Masses of worms may be expelled in feces and these worms should be taken to your vet for examination.

**Treatment**

The drug of choice for most herps is fenbendazole at 75 mg per kg body weight given orally once with an additional treatment 7 to 10 days later. Pyrantel pamoate at 12 mg per kg given once by mouth is a secondary

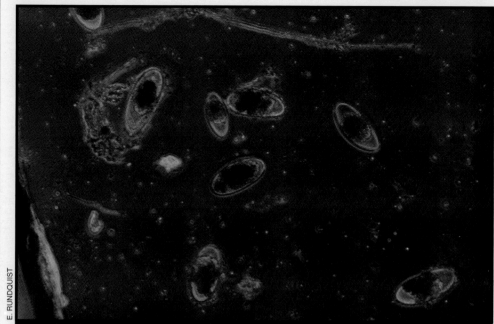

E. RUNDQUIST

Oxyurids, otherwise known as pinworms, are fairly common in reptiles, and usually do not cause any great harm unless they occur in large numbers. Insect-eating lizards are commonly affected, and if any of your own stock is tested positive for pinworms, you should re-evaluate their foodstuffs. Photo of an oxyurid ova from an insectivorous lizard.

choice as is mebendazole at 25 mg per kg, again given once orally. For turtles, the easiest drug to give is levamisol phosphate at 8 mg per kg given SQ or IM with an additional treatment two weeks later. Post-treatment fecal exams should be done after two weeks. Additional treatments may be necessary as hooks can occasionally be quite persistent, especially in turtles. NOTE: If you keep any herbivorous reptile outside for any length of time, they should be tested for hooks at least three times per year. This recommendation also applies to strongyles.

## PINWORMS (OXYURIDS)

Pinworms are one of the few nematodes with which people in developed countries may be familiar, as they are fairly common in children and are quite irritating, both physically and psychologically. However, reptile pinworms, as far as I know, are not transmissible to people. Pinworms are especially common in insect-eating lizards, but can be found in any reptile. I am unaware of their occurrence in amphibians. Pinworms usually do not cause serious illness in herps, but, as with people, heavy loads may be irritating. As these worms have a direct life cycle, reinfection may occur if good husbandry is not practiced. As noted earlier, domestic crickets may be a source of pinworm infection. If your animals test positive repeatedly for pinworms, it is a good idea to have your food source checked out for pinworms also. If the food source is positive, you might want to consider getting your crickets from another source. Lab mice may also carry pinworms.

### Diagnosis

Positive diagnosis is made by fecal flotation examination. Very small worms may be present in feces.

### Treatment

The drug of choice is thiabendazole at 100 mg per kg given once orally. Ivermectin at 200 mcg per kg given once SQ is also effective. Follow-up fecal exams should be conducted two weeks after the initial treatment. Additional treatments may be necessary.

## LUNGWORMS (*RHABDIAS*)

Lungworms are a particular bane of wild frogs and toads and are quite common in wild-caught poison dart frogs (dendrobatids). They can and do cause serious illness. However, treatment, especially in such small frogs as dendrobatids, is problematic. Treatment is difficult in these animals for two reasons. First, it is difficult to determine accurate dosages of drugs for such small frogs and, if an oral medication is used, the stress of administration may kill a debilitated frog or the jaws may be broken when trying to pry the mouth open to inject the drug. Second, and this is the most serious problem, frogs with heavy lungworm infections may die after treatment as the worms killed by the treatment may

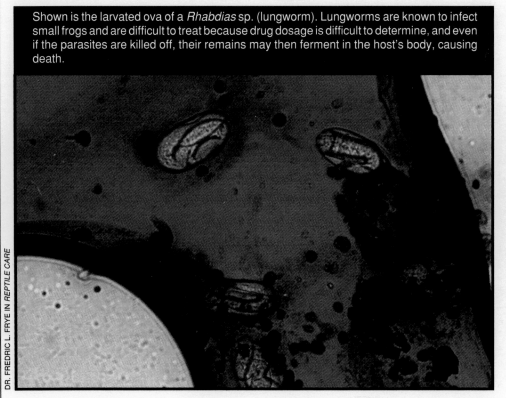

Shown is the larvated ova of a *Rhabdias* sp. (lungworm). Lungworms are known to infect small frogs and are difficult to treat because drug dosage is difficult to determine, and even if the parasites are killed off, their remains may then ferment in the host's body, causing death.

DR. FREDRIC L. FRYE IN *REPTILE CARE*

decompose in the infected animal's body and the toxic byproducts of decomposition may kill the frog. It's a tough choice, but I would choose to attempt treatment because the lungworms will eventually kill your pet anyway. Lungworms have a direct life cycle and may be a source of infection for other frogs in your collection.

### Diagnosis

Diagnosis is made by direct fecal smear or fecal flotation examination. Very small, pale worms may be present in fecal matter and these should be taken to your vet for positive identification.

### Treatment

The drug of choice is thiabendazole and should be attempted as a first treatment. The drug should be finely powdered and dusted on food items (hatchling crickets, fruit flies, etc.) These food items should then be offered to the frog. Ivermectin at 2 mg per kg applied to the frog's back once can also be tried, but remember the warning about decomposition toxicity. If the animal survives, follow-up fecal exams should be done 10 to 14 days post-treatment. This also applies to thiabendazole treatment.

### WHIPWORMS (TRICHURIDS)

Whipworms, fortunately, are uncommon in herps. They are most frequently found in reptiles. They can cause moderate to severe illness and should always be treated on discovery. Whipworms have a direct life cycle and should be considered a source of infection for other animals in your collection.

### Diagnosis

Diagnosis is made by direct fecal smear and/or fecal floatation examination. Worms may also be passed in feces.

### Treatment

The treatment of choice for whipworms is ivermectin at 200 mcg per kg given once SQ. Fenbendazole at 75 mg per kg or mebendazole at 25 mg per kg, both given once orally, may also be effective. Post-treatment fecal exams should be done two weeks later.

### SPIRURIDS

Spirurids are found rarely in reptiles. I have seen them most often in tortoises. They are rather unusual worms and I am not sure if they cause serious illness. However, because they can be present in very large numbers and produce large numbers of eggs, they should be treated on discovery.

### Diagnosis

Positive diagnosis is made by direct fecal examination or fecal flotation.

### Treatment

A number of drugs may be effective against these worms. If your tortoise tests positive for spirurids, I would start with levamisol phosphate at 8 mg per

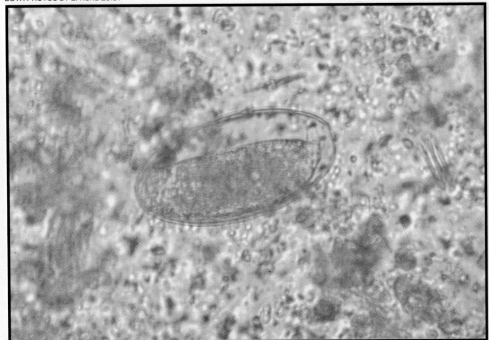

Spirurids are fairly uncommon in reptiles (virtually unknown in amphibians), and very often originate from food items. Signs of spirurid infestation is subtle and often undetectable except through direct fecal examination of fecal flotation, but the problem, once identified, can usually be eradicated with relative ease. **Above**, a spirurid egg after its 12th day of incubation. **Below**, a spirurid with eggs, found in a Leopard Tortoise, *Geochelone pardalis*.

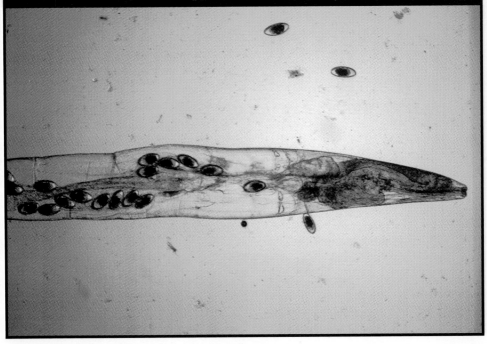

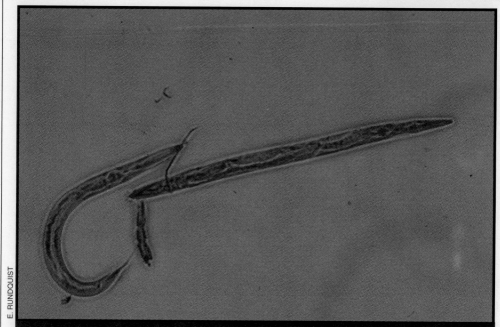

E. RUNDQUIST

Worms of the genus *Capillaria*, like the larvae shown here, taken from a Cottonmouth, *Agkistrodon piscivorus*, are not only pathogenic, making them dangerous to herps, but also highly transmissible to humans. If you have an animal infested with *Capillaria*, have it treated immediately and practice the strictest husbandry techniques.

kg given once SQ or IM. Fendendazole, at 75 mg per kg, or mebendazole, at 25 mg per kg, should be mixed into a favorite food item and given orally once. For other reptiles, ivermectin, at 200 mcg per kg, may either be given SQ or orally once. Do a follow-up fecal exam two weeks after treatment.

### *CAPILLARIA* WORMS

Worms of the genus *Capillaria* are nasty, for two reasons. They are highly pathogenic to herps and they can also be transmitted to people (direct life cycle). Most herp parasites are of no concern to people because they cannot be transmitted to people, *Capillaria* is a definite exception. These worms are most commonly seen in lizards and snakes, particularly Asian and American pit vipers (*Agkistrodon*, *Crotalus*, *Deinagkistrodon*, *Sistrurus*, *Trimeresurus*) and Asian monitor lizards (*Varanus*). If your animal tests positive for *Capillaria*, use caution when handling the infected animal and practice good hygiene. Always disinfect your tools and hands (latex gloves are advisable) after working affected animals and keep your hands away from your mouth and nose. In other words, don't pick your nose while cleaning or treating *Capillaria* infected pets. Symptoms of *Capillaria* infection in people include violent diarrhea, abdominal dissension, and pain. The symptoms are similar to hepatitis. Diagnosis for people is as for herps.

### Diagnosis

Positive diagnosis is made from direct fecal examination and fecal flotation exam.

### Treatment

The drug of choice is mebendazole at 25 mg per kg given orally once. A secondary treatment is pyrantel pamoate at 12 mg per kg given once by mouth. Start post-treatment fecal exams seven days after the initial treatment. Additional treatments may be necessary.

Well, that's it for nematodes. The next sections will cover some of the lesser lights of the worm world: tapeworms (cestodes), flukes (trematodes), acanthocephalans, and pentastomes.

## TAPEWORMS

Tapeworms are uncommon in herps, adult stages being found mostly in snakes. I make reference to adults as herps are also prime intermediate vectors for certain larval stages of tapeworms (tapeworms have an indirect life cycle). These intermediate forms are particularly common in frogs and certain snakes and are difficult to diagnose and even more difficult to treat. Fortunately, these larvae do not appear to cause any problems, for the most part. Adult tapeworms generally do not cause serious problems either, but heavy infestations may block the gut or interfere with adequate nutrient uptake in the host. Larval forms migrating through

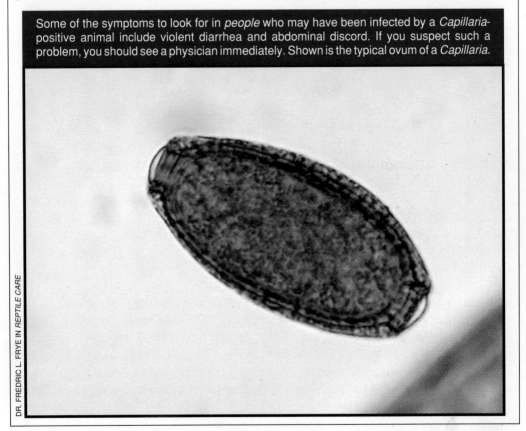

Some of the symptoms to look for in *people* who may have been infected by a *Capillaria*-positive animal include violent diarrhea and abdominal discord. If you suspect such a problem, you should see a physician immediately. Shown is the typical ovum of a *Capillaria*.

DR. FREDRIC L. FRYE IN *REPTILE CARE*

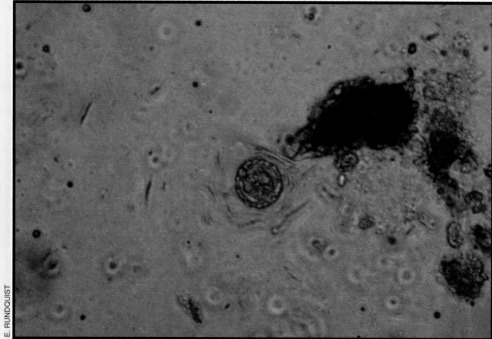

E. RUNDQUIST

Tapeworms are found in a number of herps, usually in their larval stage since herptiles often serve as intermediate vectors. However, particularly heavy "tape" infestations can cause blockage of the gut or interfere with nutritional intake. Photo of a tapeworm ova found in a Boa Constrictor, *Boa constrictor*.

the body wall may cause peritonitis, although I have never seen such problems. These migrating larvae are most commonly seen in Asian arboreal snakes (which frequently feed on frogs, a prime vector). Tapes are also found in a number of lizards, particularly monitors. Wild-caught Water Monitors (*Varanus salvator*) are especially prone to tapeworm infection. Captive-bred reptiles may also be infected with the mouse tapeworm (*Hymenolepis*) from domestic mice. The mouse tapeworm can cause serious illness in animals it infects and should be treated immediately on discovery. As with many potential parasite carriers, make sure your food sources are prime and come from clean stock.

**Diagnosis**

Positive diagnosis is made by direct fecal smear or fecal floatation examination. Tapeworm sections may also be passed in feces. They look like thin, very flat white ribbons. These sections should be taken to your vet for positive identification. Lumps beneath the skin in arboreal, frog-eating snakes may indicate the presence of migrating tapeworm larvae.

**Treatment**

A highly effective drug for tapeworms is praziquantel at 10 mg per kg body weight given orally once. Other drugs which have been used successfully are niclosamide and bunamidine hydrochloride. The dosage for the former is 159 mg per kg and for the latter is 25 to 50 mg per kg. Be aware that these latter two drugs are relatively toxic and they should be used judiciously. In addition, bunamidine should never be used in an animal with a known heart condition. Although reptilian cardiology is pretty much unknown, if your animal is grossly obese (which is fairly common in captive herps. If some is good, more is better, right?), you should assume a heart condition and use praziquantel. Additional treatments may be necessary, as adult tapes are tough and notoriously difficult to kill.

If sparganosis (those subdermal lumps I mentioned) is diagnosed, the larvae can be removed surgically. Several such minor surgeries may be necessary as larvae continue to migrate. Your animal should also be treated with tapeworm drugs.

## FLUKES (CESTODES)

Flukes are relatively uncommon in herps. They are most commonly seen in anurans, aquatic turtles, and aquatic snakes (especially American garter and ribbon snakes and water snakes [*Thamnophis* and *Nerodia*]). They may occur in any frog-eating herp and can be found in terrestrial turtles that are kept outside and feed on native vegetation. I have observed that the latter case is prevalent in the central U.S. Flukes have an indirect life cycle.

Fluke treatment is problematic in that it depends on where the

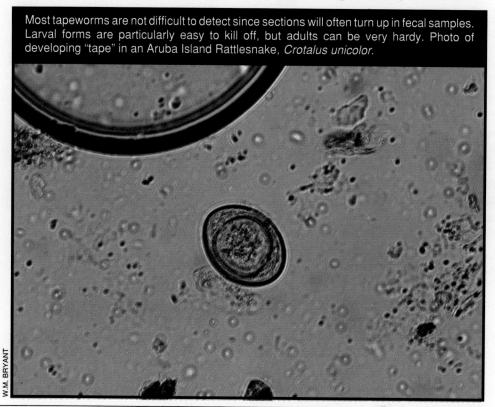

Most tapeworms are not difficult to detect since sections will often turn up in fecal samples. Larval forms are particularly easy to kill off, but adults can be very hardy. Photo of developing "tape" in an Aruba Island Rattlesnake, *Crotalus unicolor*.

W.M. BRYANT

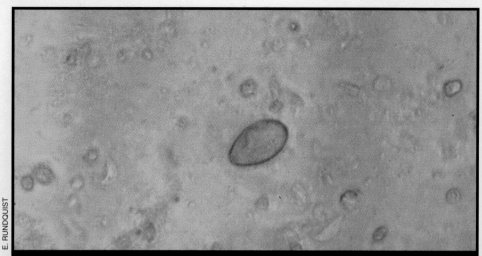

E. RUNDQUIST

Flukes are not very common in herptiles. They do turn up in land-dwelling turtles that feed on vegetation, and also in North American natricines such as the garter and ribbon snakes, *Thamnophis*, and the water snakes, *Nerodia*. There are a number of different types of flukes and can be found in different areas of the host's body. Some apparently are relatively harmless while others are potentially deadly. Shown is a fluke ovum found in a Water Monitor, *Varanus salvator*.

parasite has taken up residence. The flukes most commonly seen in aquatic snakes are found in the mouth and are easily observed. They do not appear to be pathogenic. Flukes may also be found in the gut. Again, these flukes do not appear to cause serious disease. Liver flukes and schistosome-like flukes, on the other hand, present major problems. Liver flukes cause major damage to the organ and, as with lungworms, killing the parasite may also kill the host due to decomposition toxicity. Schistosome-like flukes are blood parasites and are a major source of parasite disease in humans. Although I am unaware of their presence in herps, they are transmitted by certain tropical flies which also feed on herps, especially crocodilians. Because flukes require at least one intermediate host, they are not

readily transmissible to other animals in your collection. However, be aware that live frogs are prime intermediate hosts for certain flukes. If you feed frogs to any of your captives, especially snakes, be sure to hard freeze the food animal(s) for at least two weeks prior to offering as food. This should kill any fluke larvae that the frog may be harboring.

Fluke disease presents no apparent physical symptoms other than the host may be inappetent and waste over a long period.

Four faces of the tapeworm. **Above left** is a whole worm, found in the intestine of a Boa Constrictor, *Boa constrictor*. **Above right** shows the rostrum of a tapeworm. Visible is the rosette of hooklets. **Bottom left** displays a tapeworm in the intestine of its host, another Boa Constrictor, which it killed. Finally, on the **bottom right**, is a typical segment of an adult tapeworm, *Spirometra europiae*. All photos by Dr. Fredric L. Frye in *Reptile Care*.

### Diagnosis

Mouth flukes appear as clusters of dark brown or black worms about 3 mm in length located in the rear of the mouth. Other flukes are diagnosed by direct fecal smear or fecal sedimentation examination. Unlike many other worms, fluke eggs do not show up readily in fecal flotations, so it is important that sedimentation tests be run if you suspect fluke infections. In areas of known fluke infestation and where you keep your animals outside, it is a good idea to run fecal sedimentation tests before releasing your pets outdoors and at the end of the outdoor season.

### Treatment

Mouth flukes are easily removed with a pair of fine forceps. Several removals may be necessary to eliminate the pest. Treatment of other flukes is more problematic. Praziquantel at 10 mg/kg body weight given once orally has been used with apparent success in getting rid of gut flukes. In the only case of gut flukes I have encountered, this treatment was successful. Liver flukes and schistosome-like flukes present other problems, as previously noted. Some workers extol the virtues of praziquantel for liver flukes. This treatment may have some merit, but I have had no experience with it. Rafoxanide has been used successfully for flukes in birds and is worth investigating for herps. Organic trivalent antimonial compounds are used to treat schistosomes in humans and, again, merit a try if you discover schistosome-like flukes in your captives. As the use of either of these kinds of drugs in herps is experimental, I cannot make particular recommendations as to dosage or regime. Rafoxanide and trivalent antimonials are both very toxic drugs, especially the antimonials. If antimonials are used, they should be given in small doses over a two to six week period.

### THORNY-HEADED WORMS (ACANTHOCEPHALANS)

Acanthocephalans interest biologists for a couple of reasons. Their appearance is bizarre, as the head of the beast is covered with multiple rows of hooks, hence their name. Also, they are believed to be a very old group of creatures that, like most parasites, had a free-living stage many millions of years ago. They apparently evolved from a free-living state to their current parasitic condition. In fact, some people think that acanthocephalans may be among the very first creatures to evolve a parasitic life style. Thorny-headed worms have an indirect life cycle, so transmission to other animals in your collection is unlikely.

Ancient history and appearance aside, acanthocephalans cause serious illness in reptiles. I have not seen any cases in amphibians, but, as thorny-heads are not very host specific, they do occur in wild frogs and the like. Fortunately, thorny-heads are rare. I have seen them most often in ground iguanas (*Cyclura*). Symptoms of

BOTH PHOTOS BY DR. FREDRIC L. FRYE IN *REPTILE CARE*

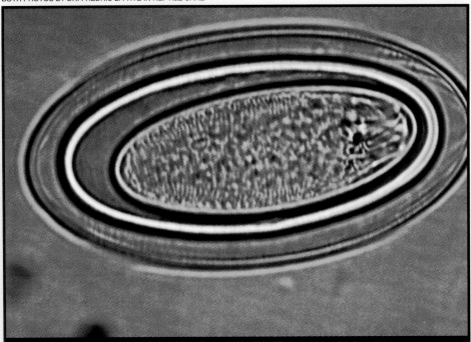

Acanthocephalans are also known as "thorny-headed worms" due to the numerous rows of hooks found on their heads. **Above** is the typical acanthocephalan ovum. **Below**, an adult worm attached to the gut of its reptilian host.

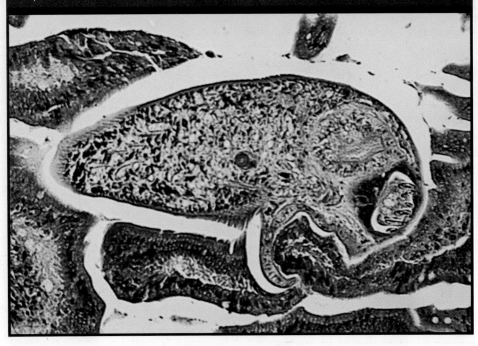

infection are much like those for hookworms: diarrheic stools that may be tinged with blood, inability of the host to gain weight or moderate weight loss.

### Diagnosis

Positive diagnosis is made by direct fecal smear examination or fecal sedimentation (as with flukes, acanthocephalan eggs do not readily float) that reveals the unusual double-walled egg that contains an embryo.

### Treatment

Pyrantel pamoate at 12 mg per kg body given once orally has been effective. Secondary options are mebendazole at 25 mg per kg given once orally with a follow-up treatment one week later or levamisol phosphate at 8 mg per

kg given once SQ. Follow-up fecal exams should be conducted at two weeks post-treatment.

### TONGUE WORMS (PENTASTOMES, LINGUATULIDS)

Tongue worms are another uncommon, unusual herp parasite. Although classified as a degenerate arachnid (spider-like) at one time, they now appear to be most closely related to crustaceans. On direct observation, it is hard to make a connection between these pale, worm-like parasites and a shrimp, but that is the apparent relationship. Truth is stranger than fiction, especially in biology.

Tongue worms are cause for concern for two reasons. They cause serious illness in herps and they are readily transmissible to

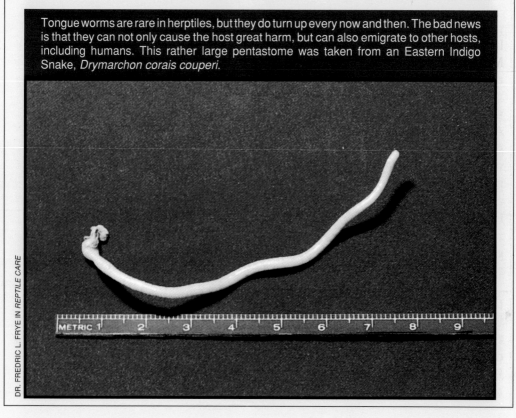

Tongue worms are rare in herptiles, but they do turn up every now and then. The bad news is that they can not only cause the host great harm, but can also emigrate to other hosts, including humans. This rather large pentastome was taken from an Eastern Indigo Snake, *Drymarchon corais couperi*.

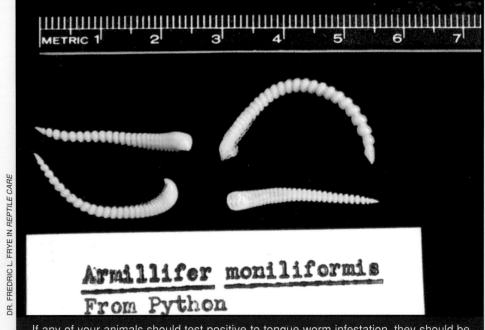

Armillifer moniliformis

From Python

If any of your animals should test positive to tongue worm infestation, they should be quarantined immediately, treated as soon as possible, and all their implements either destroyed or sterilized. Furthermore, you as the keeper should be tested for an infestation of your own. Treatment of tongue worms in humans is painful and often ineffective.

people, having a direct life cycle. In fact, snakes (particularly Middle Eastern vipers and rattlesnakes) are the major reservoir for these worms and the source of many human infections. Asian lizards are another reservoir source. Use extreme caution in working your pet if it tests positive for pentastomes. The animal should be immediately isolated and it should be the animal you work last. Wear latex gloves when handling the animal and destroy the gloves afterwards. Always disinfect the holding unit, tools, and your hands. Do not touch your face until you have thoroughly washed and disinfected your hands. Prevention is critical in that treatment for people is painful,

difficult, and usually not highly effective. Although the possibility of disease transmission from herps to people is highly overrated in some quarters (bordering on hysteria in some cases), tongue worms present a very real threat to people and I cannot emphasize enough being careful when working with infected animals.

**Diagnosis**

Diagnosis is problematic. Adult worms may occasionally be observed in the mouth or expelled from the lungs. Direct fecal smear examination may reveal pentastome eggs. Hosts do not usually present clear symptoms of infection and many times the presence of the parasite is revealed only upon autopsy.

## Treatment

Another tough one. Disethylcarbamazine has been suggested as a possible treatment but I have not had any experience with the drug. Ivermectin at 200 mcg to kg body given once SQ with a follow-up treatment one week later does appear to be effective. However, as with liver flukes, be aware that decomposing worms may set up a toxic shock syndrome. Since these large parasites live in either the nasal cavities, lungs, or tissues which connect the gut organs, surgery may be the only effective treatment.

## IN CONCLUSION

I hope the preceding accounts have been of some use to you in helping to keep your animals in peak condition. As noted previously, you can avoid many parasite problems by acquiring captive-bred and born animals. When purchasing a new pet, you should always inquire as to the origins of the animal. Although wild-caught animals may be cheaper in some cases and may appear to be in good condition, they are less than ideal candidates for captivity because of possible pre-existing health conditions and because they are under considerable stress in their new environment. This stress will almost invariably exacerbate any pre-existing conditions. Remember that even domestic herps, such as the ubiquitous Corn Snake (*Elaphe guttata*), are still basically wild animals emotionally and just being held in captivity is a stressor.

Regardless of the origin of your pets, the very first thing you should do after acquisition is to have your vet run fecal checks on them. If the first analysis is negative, you should have at least one (preferably two) other tests done at weekly intervals afterwards. For animals that test positive and are treated, you should always do post-treatment follow-up checks and these animals should be checked quarterly for at least one year until you get consistent negative results. As I pointed out before, some parasites can be difficult to get rid of or to detect. New acquisitions should always be quarantined for 30 to 60 days (longer is better) before they are introduced to other animals in your collection. Any animal that shows signs of disease should be routinely checked for parasites as well as other disease sources.

Always practice good hygiene when tending to your pets. One of the surest ways to pass certain parasites to other animals in your collection is by failing to clean and disinfect properly. This means for every holding unit, every time. That may sound tedious (and for large collections, it is tedious. Take if from someone who has maintained hundreds of herps at a time), but you will save yourself a lot of headaches (and your animals a lot of pain) by being consistent in your cleaning methods. Done properly, good hygiene doesn't really take that much extra effort.

Always work with a veterinarian

BOTH PHOTOS BY W. P. MARA

It cannot be stressed enough that the best way to handle any health problems in reptiles and amphibians is to avoid them in the first place, and some of the best techniques for doing this include carefully evaluating food items so as to cut down the risk of endoparasitic invasion (many of which being with the foodstuffs) and closely examining every external inch of your pets in order to spot any developing ectoparasitics. **Above**, a Northwestern Garter Snake, *Thamnophis ordinoides*, takes a piece of trout that was boiled and cooled, then treated with a vitamin/mineral powder. **Below**, the scales of a healthy (and gravid) Red-spotted Garter Snake, *Thamnophis sirtalis concinnus*.

in undertaking any diagnosis or treatment of parasite problems. Although I realize that many anti-parasitic drugs can be obtained without a veterinarian's authorization, you should never undertake treatment on your own, even if you think you know exactly what the problem is. Treating prophylactically without determining whether or not a problem may be present is not only poor medicine, it is just plain stupid in most cases. Many of these drugs are toxic and only a vet is in a position to determine and evaluate an effective course of treatment. Indeed, in some countries (such as Britain), only veterinarians are legally authorized to determine animal disease and treatment for same. Remember, the diagnoses and treatments I have suggested herein are only that, suggestions. Many new veterinary medications are developed each year and vets are usually aware of these new drugs, their effects, effectiveness, proper treatment regimes, and side effects. If your vet is unfamiliar with herp medicine (and that is likely in some areas), you might want to show him this booklet or have her or him acquire a copy for use in helping them determine an effective course of treatment for your pet. All of the drugs and regimes suggested herein have been tested on herps by licensed veterinarians and were developed in consultation with veterinarians.

Although there is a tendency by folks to assume that amphibians and reptiles (especially the latter) are pretty hardy critters, in reality they are not ideal captives for the most part and may in fact be quite delicate. Herps are not next-to-maintenance-free captives, no matter what someone may have told you. That cute little wild-caught Ball Python (*Python regius*) of yours may have grave, unapparent health problems that only a vet can properly diagnose. You have a serious responsibility when keeping these animals and they deserve the same veterinary considerations as any other pet. If you are not willing to make the same commitment to a frog as you would to a dog or cat, then you should not be keeping it. As many herps (reptiles in particular) may live in captivity for 30 years or more with proper care, your commitment may not be short term. You should understand that before acquiring any amphibian or reptile. Herps are not some unusual sort of prize to be stuck in an aquarium and displayed to your friends until it dies. A cheap price does not mean a cheap life. Amphibians and reptiles suffer and feel pain in much the same manner as any other creature (although their ways of expressing such may not be readily apparent) and it is your obligation to make your captives lives as pleasant as is reasonably possible.

Plumpness is something to look for in an animal you're thinking of purchasing. Notice the well-proportioned body of this healthy Red-spotted Newt, *Notophthalmus viridescens viridescens*. It does not boast the characteristic "hunger folds" (also visible on the sides and along the vertebra) common to many animals suffering from inappetance. Photo by W. P. Mara.

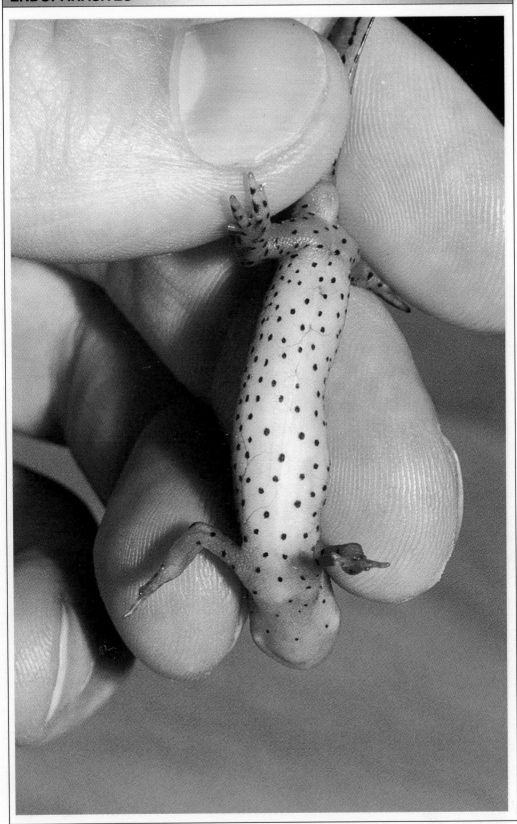

All in all, estimating an animal's health is, at best, only a guess until it can be brought to a vet for thorough examination. This Grandis Day Gecko, *Phelsuma madagascariesnsis grandis*, for example, has beautiful skin tone, bright coloration, and seems to have an adequate appetite, but none of this means there are no internal problems presently in development. Appearances can indeed be deceiving.

# BIBLIOGRAPHY

Frye, Frederic L. 1981. *Biomedical and Surgical Aspects of Captive Reptile Husbandry*. Veterinary Medical Publishing Company. 456 pp.

Frye, Frederic L. 1991. *Reptile Care*. T. F. H. Publications, Inc. 2 volumes. 652 pp.

Kauffeld, Carl. 1969. *Snakes: The Keeper and the Kept*. Doubleday and Company, Inc. 248 pp.

Letcher, James, and Michael Glade. "Efficacy of ivermectin as an anthelminthic in leopard frogs." Journal of the Association of Veterinary Medicine 200(4): 537-538.

Mattison, Christopher. 1982. *The Care of Reptiles and Amphibians in Captivity*. Blandford Press, England. 304 pp.

Murphy, James B. 1975. *A Brief Outline of Suggested Treatments for Diseases of Captive Reptiles*. Society for the Study of Amphibians and Reptiles, Herpetological Circular No. 1: 1-13

Murphy, James B., and Joseph T. Collins, eds. 1980. *Reproductive Biology and Diseases of Captive Reptiles*. Society for the Study of Amphibians and Reptiles Contribution to Herpetology No. 1: 277 pp.

Murphy, James B., and Joseph T. Collins. 1983. *A Review of the Diseases and Treatment of Captive Turtles*. AMS Publishing, Lawrence, Ks.: 56 pp.

Reichenbach-Klinke, H., and E. Elkan. 1965. *Diseases of Amphibians*. T. F. H. Publications, Inc.

Reichenbach-Klinke, H., and E. Elkan. 1965. *Diseases of Reptiles*. T. F. H. Publications, Inc.

Rundquist, Eric M. 1994. *Reptiles and Amphibians: Management in Captivity*. T. F. H. Publications, Inc. 220 pp.

Sloss, M. W., and R. L. Kemp. 1978. *Veterinary Clinical Parasitology*. Iowa State University Press, Ames, Iowa.

Weigel, John. *Care of Australian Reptiles in Captivity*. Reptile Keepers Association, New South Wales, Australia. 144 pp. Zimmerman, H. 1979. *Tropical Frogs*. T. F. H. Publications, Inc. 93 pp.

# SUGGESTED READING

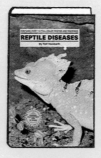

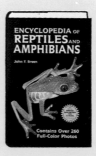

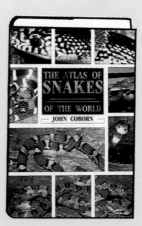

These and thousands of other animal books have been published by TFH. TFH is the world's largest publisher of animal books. You can find our titles at the same place you bought this one, or write to us for a free catalog.

# INDEX

Page numbers in **boldface** refer to illustrations.

# INDEX

Page numbers in **boldface** refer to illustrations.